# Lemonade Laughter & Laid-Back Joy

## Becky Freeman

**HARVEST HOUSE PUBLISHERS**
Eugene, Oregon 97402

*Published in association with the literary agency of Alive Communications, Inc., 7680 Goddard Street, Suite 200, Colorado Springs, CO 80920*

*Cover by Koechel Peterson & Associates, Minneapolis, Minnesota*

**Advisory:** Readers are advised to consult with their physician or other medical practitioner before implementing the suggestions that follow. This book is not intended to take the place of sound medical advice or to treat specific maladies. Neither the author nor the publisher assumes any liability for possible adverse consequences as a result of the information contained herein.

**LEMONADE LAUGHTER AND LAID-BACK JOY**
Copyright © 2001 by Becky Freeman
Published by Harvest House Publishers
Eugene, Oregon 97402

Library of Congress Cataloging-in-Publication Data
Freeman, Becky, 1959–
    [View from the porch swing]
    Lemonade laughter and laid-back joy / Becky Freeman.
        p. cm.
    Originally published: A view from the porch swing. Nashville: Broadman & Holman, ©1998.
    ISBN 0-7369-0647-9
    1. American wit and humor.    I. Title.
PN6162.F744    2001
814'.54—dc21                                                   2001024265

**Printed in the United States of America**

01  02  03  04  05  06  07  / BP-CF /  10  9  8  7  6  5  4  3  2  1

*To Gene and Carol Kent,*
*whose encouragement continually inspires my heart,*
*and whose lives are living examples of Christ's love*

## Acknowledgments

Many thanks to my family, my friends, Harvest House Publishers, and Greg Johnson for bringing new life to this book that has been so dear to my heart.

# Contents

## Part IV
## Down-Home Hints to Health & Happiness

*A Potpourri of Laid-Back Musings*

## Part V
## Green Pastures, Still Waters

*Answers That Restore the Soul*

# Porch Swing Jubilee

'm in love with porches. Front, back, wraparound—you name it, they are my friends. Ditto for backyard decks and boat docks, treetops and river rocks. They're wonderful places to ponder, or to shell a peck of black-eyed peas. Great surroundings, these, to do what our grandmothers called "settin' a spell" or we young-'uns call "vegging out."

Ah...the porch swings I've known. And what those porch swings could say if they were the gossiping sort! Yes, the prime spot for "settin' and shellin' and mendin'" will always be, to me, the Great American Porch Swing. In fact, a few years back, when my mind was in dire need of some heavy-duty emotional mending, I skipped the mental hospital and came out swinging' instead. Maybe I should back up and explain.

It all began a few years ago, on a day when my mother drove out for a visit to our home in the country...

The afternoon unfolded sun-kissed and lazy. Because Mother had retired from writing, we had no book business to discuss, no agenda planned out. For both of us, I think, it was remarkably fun just to hang out together on this autumn afternoon.

Observing my mother's tiny figure tucked neatly into her slim-fitting jeans, I thought to myself, *I can't believe Mother's almost 60—she's still so attractive and full of spunk.*

We sank onto my red plaid couch, each of us sipping at our warm mugs of tea. Then I began to really unwind, pouring out my thoughts of late—sharing from the secret corners of my mind, where the Really Big Ideas seem to pool and simmer. It was one of those times when I let my words flow unchecked, chaff and grain alike, like falling leaves on a velvet breeze. Mostly, I'd been pondering variations on one simple question: How can I live out the rest of my days with a greater sense of laid-back joy (as opposed to my accustomed high-gear stress)?

Man, I was on a philosophical roll, a mental runaway train. When I finally paused to draw breath, Mother gave a deliberate nod of her wise silver head.

"I know exactly what you mean," she said. *She did?*

"You do?" my words echoed the thought. Perhaps I was not an alien life-form after all.

"Oh yeah," Mother declared. Then she placed her cup on the coffee table so she could gesture freely. "It's just like I felt the other day when I was watching an old rerun of *The Andy Griffith Show.* There was a scene of Barney and Andy sitting on the front porch swing, chatting and chuckling and stopping here and there to sigh at the stars. Something inside of me leapt, and I thought to myself, *We aren't—as a people—doing enough sitting and swinging and shooting the breeze any more.*

"Mother! You are brilliant!" I exclaimed, feeling as though she'd just handed me the Secret to the Universe. "That's *it!* I want to swing on the porch—glide back and forth in rapport with my husband and kids and friends. I want to prop one leg up, lie back, look at the stars—and shoot the breeze with the One who made them, y'know what I mean? I want to slow down, simplify, be more at home in my own head. To live life with laid-back joy. What I need is a Mayberry of Soul!"

As part of my quest for a Mayberry Mind, almost every morning I began taking half an hour, sometimes more, to rock my soul in the bosom of our back porch bench. Instead of dragging myself back to bed whenever I was hit with the blues, I came out swinging instead.

After a few weeks of this rockin' ritual, I suddenly realized how much more joyful and refreshed, rested and balanced I was beginning to feel (that is, as balanced as a woman "so right-brained she pulls to the right and walks in circles" can ever hope to be). I was on a real upswing (pardon the pun), even thinking at times I might die from an overdose of contentment.

Sometime later, as I was reading in the Old Testament, I stumbled across an ancient God-given formula for maintaining the well-being of the Earth and its inhabitants. In Leviticus 25, the Israelites were told to take a special Time-Out, an entire year in fact, for rest and refocusing—the Jubilee. Even the soil was to be left alone to sleep and renew itself. Suddenly, the reason I was experiencing a personal blooming of my own became clear. There's a certain type of replenishment that is needed for growth, and without realizing it consciously, I'd been steadily taking in just the sort of nourishment my body, soul, and mind had been hungering for. A human life, like soil that's farmed intensively, needs regular times to lie fallow so it can recharge and function well.

After the end of my own personal season of jubilee, I wrote a book about all I had learned and called it *Porch Swing Jubilee* (though it ended up being published under the title *A View from the Porch Swing*). The writing of that book ushered me into a new way of thinking, feeling, and coping with my emotions, my spiritual life, and my relationships. Now, when I speak on the subject of Porch Swing Peace, I tell my audiences, "In many ways, I divide my life into 'B.P.S' and 'A.P.S'—or 'Before Porch Swing' and 'After Porch Swing.'"

Rose, my able assistant and incredible friend, reminded me the other day of an incident that occurred at a conference (put on by Hearts at Home) where I was speaking to—gulp—5000 mommies of young children. They were the best audience ever because they were simply so grateful for an hour when they could sit alone in a cushioned theater chair, unencumbered by a nursing baby or whining toddler. I could have sneezed and they'd have found it uproariously funny, quoted from the dictionary and they'd have been sure I was delivering wisdom from above.

After speaking, I wound my way to the book tables and found one woman standing in line and clutching a worn copy of *A View from the Porch Swing* in one hand and a Kleenex in the other. Tearfully she wrapped her arms around my neck and said, "Thank you."

I hugged her and said, "Well, bless you, sweet lady. What are you thanking me for?"

"Thank you for writing this book," she explained. "I kid you not, I tell everyone that it's my Prozac. I was spiraling down the drain with postpartum blues and heading to get a prescription for an antidepressant. But I happened upon your book at the bookstore, and something about the swing on the front...drew me in. I never got the prescription filled because I got so sidetracked with reading. Chapter by chapter I found myself relaxing, laughing, giving up my struggle for perfection, and by the time I finished, the depression had simply lifted. As you can see, I've turned to it again and again when my spirits have needed a little lift."

When we receive help during a time of great pain, the ultimate joy is not only in surviving the crisis ourselves, but in passing on to others the comfort we've been given. It is, perhaps, the best feeling God gives us humans on Planet

Earth. So I was at least as grateful to that woman for sharing her story with me and blessing my day as she was for my having written the book.

Perhaps more than with any of my other books, the mail I've received from readers of *Porch Swing* has been profound. "You've given me my life—and my laugh—back." "I'll never look at life in the same pressure-cookered way again." One therapist gives the book to her clients as an exit present—something to help them transition from the cocoon of therapy to the world of real life.

And so, when my editor called and said, "Becky, I hate to make this phone call, but we are taking *Porch Swing* out of print," I mumbled back, "It's okay, really. It had to happen sometime." Then I went to bed and cried. I felt as though my book baby had died a premature death. What would I give to people who were hurting? What book would I share with those who wanted to live with more laid-back joy? My books on marriage, motherhood, and friendship were all relationship-oriented and in a different category altogether. *Porch Swing* was my Heart's Declaration—of my Independence from Perfection.

Then a few months later, some wonderful editors at Harvest House Publishers became as enthused as I was about the original book and decided it deserved a second life, with a fresh title and a brand-new cover. So you are holding in your hands *Lemonade Laughter and Laid-Back Joy,* my Declaration, now with a new look and updated stories and thoughts.

So that's the story behind the story about to unfold before you.

If the day is pretty, I urge you to grab some lemonade and head outside to a rocker or porch swing.

Then settle back, open your Paperback Prozac, and follow me in the search for a life of laid-back joy.

**What a happy year it will be! ... For it is a holy Year of Jubilee for you.**

LEVITICUS 25:11,12 TLB

# Part I

# Cashing Out
# to the Country!

*A Complicated Search
for the Simple Life*

# 1

# Cappuccino Cowboys

I am constantly amazed and amused by this life I'm now leading—so far removed from the one I once knew.

A few years ago, I drove up to the high school with my 13-year-old daughter, Rachel. I asked her to run over and give a sports drink to her older brother, Zeke, who was about to begin an after-school session of football practice. She soon returned, breathlessly diving into the front seat.

"So Rachel, that was fast," I commented. "Did you give Zeke the Gatorade?"

"No," she responded calmly, "I gave it to Goof."

"Pardon me?"

"I gave it to Goof Fry and told him to give it to Zeke."

"Hold it. Are you telling me there is a child who goes by the name of 'Goof' at your school?"

"Yep. It's what everyone calls him."

"Even the teachers?"

"Mo-*ther,* yes! Everybody calls him that—the teachers, his parents, the whole school. Nobody ever thinks about it being strange or anything. He's Ida Lou's brother."

Scratching my head, I said, "So let me get this straight. There are a pair of siblings in your school named Goof and Ida Lou Fry."

"Yes."

I grinned. Rachel, eyeing me suspiciously, asked, "What are you smiling about?"

"Oh," I replied, "I just love country life, that's all."

On our way home, Rachel and I stopped off at the local grocery store to pick up a couple of hot barbeque sandwiches and some cold Dr Peppers. There, lying on the counter was a flyer from the taxidermist next door. "This is too good," I said aloud as I scanned the paper. Here, in brief, are the actual contents of the flyer.

### Varmint Tournament

Bobcats 100 points

Coyotes 50 points

Big cat and big coyote judged by weight, not by length

All animals entered in contest will be
checked thoroughly to verify fresh kills

Let's keep this an honest and fun event

*How would one go about cheating in a varmint contest?*
I wondered. *What?—do some unscrupulous hunters try to
fluff up road kill and pass it off as a freshly killed varmint?*

I haven't always been surrounded by bobcats, coyotes, and road kill—or people with names like Joe Bob, Linda Sue, Goof, and Ida Lou.

Actually, I grew up in the suburbia of *The Wonder Years*—complete with cul-de-sac, Country Squire station wagon, coppertone appliances, and a hot pink, orange, and yellow daisied bedroom. But even back in the groovy '60s and the mod '70s, I longed for a simpler country-style life. While my friends dreamed of being models in New York

City, I pictured myself growing up to look like Mary Ann from *Gilligan's Island*. In my daydreams it was always a spring morning. I would be wearing a red-and-white gingham dress, singing as I fed the chickens in front of my farmhouse—surrounded by white picket fences, tweeting birds, and Jersey cows lowing in the distance.

Though I did turn out to look somewhat like Mary Ann (only slightly more "well-rounded"), my most favorite TV role model was actually blonde, pigtailed Elly May Clampett from *The Beverly Hillbillies*. I sincerely thought she was one of the prettiest, sweetest girls on TV, and I was determined to grow up to be just like her. (In a fun twist of fate—yesterday I was at the National Religious Broadcasters convention and there was ELLY MAY! She's many years older but still beautiful, her long, soft, blonde tresses pulled back in a loose braid. She was gracious and kind, and loves Jesus, too. It's so nice to see a child star turn out to be as sweet in real life as you once thought she was.)

By the time I was 14, I knew every single one of John Denver's country-praisin', back-home-again songs by heart (I must confess, I still do). I especially liked the one he sang about blowin' up the TV and movin' to the country and raisin' kids on peaches. Then I fell in love with Scott Freeman—who, at 16, looked a lot like John Denver did: straight sandy bangs, square jaw, wide smile, and wire-rimmed glasses.

Though we lived in the 'burbs, my parents hung a rustic porch swing in the back yard, where Scott and I did our share of old-fashioned courting. Much to my delight, I discovered during one of our snuggly chats that Scott shared my Picket-Fence Dreams. When we married in our late teens, we could only afford a small duplex in town, but we spent many an evening planning the day when we'd break free from suburbia and head to the hills.

By the time our first two sons, Zach and Zeke, were born, we'd saved a little money toward making our dream a reality. (A very little money—a whopping three-digit figure, as I recall.) We'd buckle the boys in their car seats and drive out of the city every chance we'd get in search of our own piece of down-home paradise. I even made up a little "lookin' for a home" ditty. The kids and I would sing it at the top of our lungs as we drove winding roads around herds of cattle and rolling green pastures.

> *We wanna live way out in the counnnn - try*
> *Way out with the roosters and the frogs—*
> *We wanna live way out in the counnnn - try*
> *Way out with the milk cows and the hogs!*

(Move over, Dixie Chicks.)

We finally found our settlin' spot—a one-acre wooded tract with a pond—about 30 miles from town. Investing our meager life's savings, we proceeded to make the first of our many hayseed dreams come true: We built our own log home. Not from one of those Lincoln Log kits either; we built ours from scratch. I say "we," but actually Scott did almost all the work. My contribution was mostly chasing kids and cheering him on. Besides, I was expanding again, or as Scott would put it, "We had two kids underfoot and one in the oven."

Since graduating from college, Scott had made a living as head of his own building company. Now he found himself specializing in log construction full-time. I doubt there was ever a job more suited to a man and vice versa. To go with his log-splittin' career, Scott grew a full beard. His standard uniform became boots, jeans, and a flannel shirt—sometimes he even added red suspenders. My mother took to calling him "Dan'l" or "Abe."

For five years Scott supervised and participated in the crafting of gorgeous homes and buildings out of logs—

cedar, pine, and aspen—accented by hand-carved stair-cases, rock fireplaces, and custom-designed woodwork and cabinetry. The downside of this particular dream-come-true was that we never got to keep any of the log homes he built—we had to keep selling them to keep the bills paid in this newborn business. I remember, very distinctly, one 18-month period when we moved FIVE times. (Rachel Praise made her debut during this time of our great migrations.)

In short, the simple life we were creating was getting awfully complicated.

Then came the well. If you didn't have your own well in the country, the neighbors across the pasture might think you were nothing but city water-drinking sissies. Not one to let his family suffer shame, Scott proceeded to dig us our own bona fide country well. With much fanfare, he and his buddies hauled in and then hovered over the well-digging machine as if it were a goose about to lay the golden geyser—sure any minute they'd hit pay-water. A week later, when they finally brought the machine to a stop some-where near the earth's core, they'd at last hit genuine $H_2O$! There was whooping and hollering and all sorts of commotion going on—that is, until Scott accidentally fumbled, and a rusty wrench slipped out of his hand and disappeared down the world's longest pipe. Then it got so quiet you could have heard a pin—or in this case, a handtool—drop.

We were finally the owners of our own well, complete with running water—the PROUD owners, I will admit. However, the water that came out of our faucet was a deep shade of burnt orange. After bathing and washing all our laundry in our country-fresh well water, our family looked like a matched set of rusted tin men. So at this point in our lives, we lived in a beautiful two-story log home—but every morning we'd sheepishly walk over to the neighbors to fill up canisters with decent drinking water. Our simple life had taken yet another complex twist.

Today, at last, we own another country home and right now cannot imagine ever selling it. It's also on a wooded acre or so, near the edge of a small lake. Peaceful, scenic, serenely beautiful—though the last several years have been anything but simple. We started out, in this particular spot, a family of six in a one-bedroom, 850-square-foot cabin. (By the time of this settlement, child number four, baby Gabe had arrived.)

At one point we inherited a small windfall (actually, it was probably more like a breezefall, but to us it seemed like a fortune!), and Scott used the money to build a beautiful two-story Victorian shell AROUND the small cabin. Then we ran out of money. So for a few years thereafter, it was a lot like living behind a Hollywood stage front. We looked good to neighbors driving by, but visitors to our home would walk through the lovely front door into an empty shell of a house, then down a hall and into the old cabin where we actually lived.

Over the years, Scott continued to knock out a wall here and add on a room there until—FINALLY—more than ten years later, we have an almost normal home. ALMOST, I say, because of one unusual feature that continues to be a sore spot between my husband and me. After building and finishing out the second story to our home, Scott refused to build stairs to it. Because, "you see," he explained with the wild-eyed logic of an escaped mental patient, "there's not room for stairs and a rock-climbing wall, too."

So our family is literally climbing the walls. (A rock-climbing wall—may I just whine for a moment?—is not easy to decorate around. I venture to say that even Martha Stewart might be stumped on this one.) There's also a lean-to ladder thing I can use to get upstairs if I have to (however, teenagers live up there, so I generally prefer to avoid that area of house anyway). And then there's a climbing rope near the wall, which tends to be the most common form of descent. Most mornings our children come swinging down to breakfast like Tarzan on a vine.

I'll admit we are not your normal everyday family. Even so, I don't think we are completely alone—because few city dwellers fully realize what they are in for when they choose to "cash out to the country" and dive into the simple life.

The lifelong residents here have names for us newly countrified folk (who often end up feeling more like country-*fried* folk by the time we're settled in). They call us High-Rise Hillbillies, Bumpkin Boomers, Yokel Yuppies, and my personal favorite, Cappuccino Cowboys. Our family used to be the lone transplants out this way, but suburban refugees are popping up all over our neck of the woods now—all trying their best to homestead, unobtrusively, among the natives. Try as they may, it's impossible not to stand out. The other day—honest—I heard that one of our Cappuccino Cowboys was out baling hay wearing a neatly pressed oxford shirt, dress pants, and 250-dollar shoes, his Rolex watch glinting in the sun. In his defense, rumor has it he was wearing overalls and a cowboy hat also.

A couple of years ago, I overheard a conversation between a recently transplanted Lexus-driving, tennis-playing female and a woman who's "been born and reared in these here parts." The local woman spoke first.

"So, Hon, you oughta come out with us tonight and go coon huntin'. Ain't nothin' more fun."

"Oh, really?" the newcomer replied, touching her manicured nails to her chin. "That sounds very interesting. And what exactly do you do with the little raccoons once you've found them?"

"Why, we eat 'em," came the matter-of-fact reply. It was like eavesdropping on Elly May inviting Ivana Trump over for some "lip-smackin' victuals."

Though we have no shortage of varmints and victuals, if there is a drawback to living in a small rural town, it's that we're hard up for exciting news. The police reports are on the order of "Two sticks of gum found missing from local kindergarten teacher's desk. Suspects being held in the corner." Columnists too are scraping the bottom of the barrel to find interesting information to share in the local newspaper. I hold in my hand an actual clipping of a local column in which the writer informs the entire community that "she's been hacking up phlegm all morning." Now there's a lovely and newsworthy tidbit to digest with your morning coffee. Still, lack of excitement is a small sacrifice to make in exchange for a peaceful life lived close to nature.

Even as I look back on the complicated road we took to get to this simple life, I have to smile and say it's been worth every rusty drop of water, every log we ever laid, every coon and possum we've had for supper. (No, not *eaten* for supper. But sometimes they do wander in from the woods for a dinnertime visit.) Why? A thousand reasons, but tonight I was given just one more perfect example.

This evening Scott was working late and Zach took his brothers to the bowling alley, so I asked my daughter, Rachel, if she'd like to join me for a bite to eat at Grant's Cafe. (Side note: We have very few stores in this area—but one is called Gantt's Village Market, the other is Grant's, with an "r," Cafe. If you don't think that keeps us Yokel Yuppies tongue-tied!) Anyway, by the time we'd finished our meal, I'd visited with two waitresses. We all, of course, know each other by name. I found out that one had an awful sinus headache and offered her my sympathy, and the other had just won a free Caribbean vacation and I offered her my jealousy. I'm still worried about another waitress—the friendliest woman on earth—who wasn't on duty tonight. She's going through a pretty tough family crisis. And this doesn't even count the folks we greeted coming in and out of the restaurant during our meal.

At one point, a cowboy strode in the front door, making a public announcement to the entire restaurant: "It's comin' down a gully-washer out there!" As he shook the water from the brim of his hat, his cafe audience responded with thoughtful comments. "Sure 'nuff is." "Heard the TV weatherman say there was gonna be a frog-strangler a-comin' in." "Yep—but I never put much stock in them ol' boys." "Looks like he was right this time, though, boy howdy. Listen to that thunder!" "Yep." "Uh-huh." "Yes siree."

Rachel and I joined in the group conversation until we finished our meal, paid our check, waved goodbye to the small crowd, and ran through the rain to our car. After starting up the engine, I pulled out of the drive. That's when I did what's affectionately known around here as "a Becky." Somehow I managed to land the nose of our car face down in a muddy ditch.

Now if I'd been in the city, I'd probably still be stuck, nose down, in the mud—waiting on some tow truck, to come haul me out of my dire predicament, at $50 an hour. But not in Small Town, USA. Before I could even roll my window down, I was surrounded by able-bodied men in boots and caps, concerned women and children, and assorted pickup trucks—all standing ready to lend aid and comfort. (As they say around here, "If you don't know what you're doing in a small town, trust me, everyone else does.") The owner of the restaurant, Mr. Grant himself, came out laughing, saying, "Becky, why am I not surprised?" and donated a new rope to the cause.

Within 15 minutes I'd met four new people and shared several laughs—wondering aloud if there was ever a ditch the nose of my car hadn't met. One of the pickups lighted up the scene with its headlight beams while another one yanked on my car's back end, and in no time I was unstuck and on my way home. I don't have to depend on the kindness of strangers—because no one's a stranger in small communities like this. And isn't that, after all, what the simple life's about?

> *Now we live way out in the counnnn - try*
> *Way out with the roosters and the frogs—*
> *We live way out in the counnnn - try*
> *Way out with the milk cows and the hogs!*

(Yeeeee-haw!)

### The LORD preserves the simple...

PSALM 116:6 NKJV

# You Might Be City Folk If...

... you don't have any problems pronouncing "Worcestershire sauce" correctly.

... for breakfast, you would prefer potatoes au gratin to grits.

... you don't know what a Moon Pie is.

... you've never, ever, eaten okra.

... you eat fried chicken with a knife and fork.

... you have no idea what a polecat is.

... you don't see anything wrong with putting a sweater on a poodle.

... you would rather have your son become a lawyer than grow up to get his own TV fishing show.

... you've never planned your summer vacation around a gun and knife show.

... you think more money should go to important scientific research at your university than to the salary of the head football coach.

... you don't have at least one can of WD-40 somewhere around the house.

... the last time you smiled was when you beat someone to an on-ramp on the freeway.

... you don't have any hats in your closet that advertise feed stores.

... you can't spit out the car window without pulling over to the side of the road and stopping.

... you would never wear pink or an appliqué sweatshirt.

... you don't know what appliqué is.

... you don't know anyone with two first names (such as Joe Bob, Billy Bob, Kay Bob, Bob Bob).

... you don't have doilies, nor do you know how to make them.

... you can't do your laundry without quarters.

... none of your fur coats are homemade.

*(found on the Internet, original source unknown)*

# 2

# Peculiar Purpose

Even before we moved to the country, my life was weird. And I continue to attract a steady stream of weird circumstances. I myself am admittedly odd sometimes, but I'm about ready to accept this fate as my life work and mission.

Nearly every week I get an e-mail from a friend-fan that starts something like this, "Becky, I was really feeling down about all the problems in my life. Then I picked up your books and read about all the disasters you get yourself into (disasters you are actually able to find amusing), and I suddenly started feeling a whole lot better about myself."

Another version is, "Becky, I've always wanted to write a book or talk to large groups of women, but frankly, I've been too intimidated. But now that I've met you and read your books—shoot, I figure if somebody like you can write and speak, I sure ought to give it a try."

My own daughter, just this week, spoke to a group of 2000 teenagers at a Beta Club convention. "Honey," I asked her, "aren't you a little bit afraid of standing in front of all those teenagers and giving a speech?" After all, she had once been the most shy of little girls, not to mention that "speaking in front of a group" usually ranks just below "fear of death by slow torture" in all the standard stress surveys. But she just stared at me and said, "Mom, I've watched you give speeches a bunch of times. And you're just a plain ol' middle-aged mom. So, *duh,* what do I have to be nervous about?"

Could my deep, weighty purpose on this planet be to make things look so unintimidating that the rest of the world takes courage to venture into uncharted territory? Or perhaps I'm here simply to lighten things up. I don't know, but no matter how hard I try to be sophisticated and normal, odd things continue to happen to and around me. I comfort myself that there must be SOME divine reason for this.

For example, there was the time I decided to clean out my old station wagon (which we lovingly named "Sag") before I darted into the local mall. I hurriedly stuffed trash from the floor and seats into a plastic bag. But somewhere between my car and the mall, I must have gotten confused. For I thought I had my purse hanging from my arm, when—in reality—I was sporting a lovely plastic bag of refuse. There I was, roving the mall, conversing with salesmen and saleswomen, like one of those demented bag ladies we so often see in movies. The kind who honestly think they look quite sophisticated carrying around a bag of trash filled with straws, paper cups, and half-eaten tacos, looped daintily over one arm.

Then there was the football game where I walked into one of two unmarked bathroom doors, hoping against hope that behind Door #1 I'd find a room full of females. Instead I barged in on a row of startled men, scurrying to find their zippers. Embarrassed, I offered a quick apology and exited, grateful that, at least now, I'd be sure to go in the correct door. Entering Door #2 full of confidence, I could not believe my eyes when I spied the backs of the same startled men lined up in a row. Turns out this was one of those bathrooms with one door for an entrance and one for an exit. And I, the lucky winner, had picked both doors.

Yes, you say, but these are weird circumstances I've created myself, out of my own stupidity. What does this have to do with divine intervention? Well, I'm getting to that.

One day I was driving down the road minding my own business when, a few cars ahead of me, I saw a grocery sack fall out of the back of a pickup truck. (In Texas, you're rarely more than a car's length from a pickup.) I could see that one of the items rolling out of the sack down the highway appeared to be a bottle of shampoo.

Then, like in one of those comical chase scenes in movies, the car in front of me ran smack over that shampoo bottle, whereupon it exploded, depositing its entire contents onto my windshield.

Gabe, my then ten-year old son, was sitting in the front seat beside me. I glanced at him briefly. He said nothing, but his mouth was wide open and his eyes were darting back and forth from the windshield to me to see what I would do next. I couldn't see a thing through the bluish green muck, so I turned on my windshield wipers.

At that very moment it started to rain. No kidding. So now I had this fascinating foaming bubble bath in full swing, sliding back and forth across my windshield. The more the wipers swept, the more the bubbles foamed and multiplied. Soap lifted off and floated from the car in streams as we drove along in the sudden shower. I glanced over at Gabe once again. Still no words coming from him, but his mouth was a little bit wider, and his eyebrows were so high they'd now disappeared under his bangs. We neared home, and as I pulled into the driveway, suddenly the sun burst from behind the clouds—the rain gone as quickly as it had begun. My windshield was sparkling clean. I rolled down my window, poked my head out, and looking up in the direction of the clouds said, "Thank you, Lord, You did a great job. I don't think my windshield's ever been this clean before."

Gabe finally found his voice, but when he did it was trembling. "Mo-o-o-m," he squeaked, "do you think other kids' mothers have these kinds of things happen to them?"

All I could do was smile and shrug, and assure him that some of us are called to be peculiar people walking through peculiar circumstances—so we can make other folks feel much better about their own lives.

**The LORD hath chosen thee to be a peculiar people...**

DEUTERONOMY 14:2 KJV

## Me 'n' Einstein

The longer I live, the more I realize I'm full of a hundred contradictions. My test scores say I'm quite bright—but then, there is no IQ or SAT quiz for plain common sense. Within the span of a five-minute conversation, one friend described me as both "spiritually wise" and "hopelessly naïve." I'm curious and studious, but my children will tell you there could not be a more forgetful mother on this earth.

In coming to terms with my own dichotomies, I've drawn special comfort from observing the life of Albert Einstein. Einstein was a classic example of the creative personality: Sure, he discovered the theory of relativity, but did he ever master the use of a comb?

# 3

# Natural Woman

I am, at this moment, living every mother's fantasy. I'm all alone (going on the third day) in a rustic cabin, in the fall of the year. For these three days, I've experimented with what life might be like if I were a single woman—and a hermit. Because I got married at the tender age of 17 and went straight from being someone's daughter to being someone's wife, the ways of living alone are as foreign to me as the habits of some ancient tribe in a far-off land. I'd been wondering, especially after a succession of intense, crowded days, *What would it feel like to live in solitary isolation for a while?*

Now I know.

It's a little quiet, even a bit lonely, but on the whole—for a short time, at least—it's rather heavenly.

I find it fascinating to be preparing meals for me and me only. I've also pondered what I would I eat if I were a single chick. What would I buy at the grocery store with only my tastes in mind, left alone to munch whenever and whatever my heart (or tummy) desired?

Here are the results to that question, thus far: I've gone through half a bag of apples, half a pint of caramel dipping sauce (fat free), a bag of chocolate cookies (fat free), half a can of turkey chili, half a can of baked beans, half a can of bean dip and assorted (fat free) chips, and two small potatoes. Oh, I did have a salad and some carrots once—thrown in for good measure.

My dinnerware has consisted of one sturdy Styrofoam plate, a small empty butter tub, and a coffee mug. (These too, may I point out, are fat free.) The sole utensils in this cabin are a huge serving spoon, a fork, and a steak knife. I eat oodles of onions on everything, with nary a thought of offending anyone with bad breath. I don't even concern myself with the beans and their well-known aftereffects. Being a recluse indeed has its perks.

Another thing: There is no reason to put on makeup or even shave my legs. Who am I going to impress? Who will I rub up against? I only comb my hair to get it out of my eyes, and I secure it back with whatever's handy—I've discovered that a large chip clip or a couple of wooden clothespins work great.

I've undergone a rare transformation in these few short days. I'm becoming more than Becky of the Boonies: I'm turning into Amazon Woman. I've left the society of Women Who Run with the Poodles and joined the pack of Women Who Run with the Wolves. Yesterday I wore a shirt with a big ketchup stain—right in the middle of my stomach—all day long. Slept in it last night. Who cares about stains when it's just you 'n' the foliage?

Yesterday the most exciting thing that happened to me was that a huge praying mantis and her mate crawled atop my computer. I put them in a glass container, with the lid slightly ajar, for scientific observation. I heard somewhere that once the female is finished mating with the male she bites his head off. I guess I'll never know. When I woke up this morning, both of them were gone. Maybe they ate each other.

Actually, the subject of male-female difficulties sort of brings me to how I landed in these woods, like some displaced Goldilocks, in the first place. I'm telling everyone that I'm away to write and reflect and catch up on work (though so far there's been more "ketchup on my work" than "catch up on my work"). If the truth be known, I'm actually in exile. Two days before I landed in the wilderness, I had a semi–nervous breakdown. It worried me because I didn't think it had a thing to do with hormones. Didn't feel like hormones. Just felt as though the world was falling apart, deadlines were looming over me like monsters, and my head was about to explode.

Scott discovered me curled up in the fetal position crying and sobbing like a baby, saying over and over again, "I just can't do it all!" Another peculiar symptom: Suddenly, I was seized with an overwhelming desire to have my house clean—SPOTLESSLY clean. IMMEDIATELY! (Me, whose first book described me as the happily oblivious owner of the "dirtiest floor in America"!) Suddenly, one little sock on the floor grated on every nerve in my body. The dust on the coffee table looked as thick and deep as the sand of the Sahara. It was all so hopeless, hopeless, hopeless! But I did not think it was PMS.

Scott found me in this pitiful condition and held me with compassion, as if I were a child, in his arms. Then he immediately set to plotting how he might creatively put me in solitary confinement for a few days. To his everlasting credit (young husbands, take note) he did not mention the words "hormones" or "PMS." Wisely, he said, "Honey, what's wrong with you is that you are just plain worn out. You need time away to re-group and to catch up on sleep and your writing. There's a cabin I know of that you can use for a few days. I'll take care of the kids, you go and relax—"

"But Scott," I blubbered, wiping my tears, "I can't possibly leave you and the children—"

"Oh, but I insist, Sweetheart. Really. You need this."

"You are the most giving man I ever met. I love you so much."

"There, there," he patted my back soothingly. "Can I help you pack your suitcase right now? Warm up the engine of the car?"

That's when I started to get a little suspicious. Scott had the slightly wild look of a male praying mantis desperately trying to save his own head. Obviously this "Momma's Getaway" held significance for the kids, too. Maybe they knew instinctively that their mother was on the verge of Wild Womandom—a sight they preferred not to behold at close distance. At this point, who was I to quibble over their motives? I was ready to do anything to help relieve the pressure building inside. When I finally agreed to accept solitary confinement, it seemed as though they might give me a standing ovation.

That very afternoon I found myself cruising through the countryside amid the brilliant fall trees painted with yellow, orange, burgundy, and chocolate-brown leaves. When I arrived at the cabin, I unpacked a few things. Then, with some surprise, I realized—well, *whaddayaknow?*—that I'd miscalculated my cycle. I *had* been under the influence of hormone drop after all! Then it dawned on me, if this had been Old Testament times, under the ceremonial law I'd have been routinely exiled like this. "The impurity...will last seven days" (Leviticus 15:19).

I used to think, *How awful to be put away like you were something disgraceful, just because it was your God-ordained female time of the month!* Now, I'm beginning to see the brilliance of such a plan. Oh, I might in some way have protested the injustice of it all if I'd lived back then, but I believe it would have eventually dawned on me that this "shunning" deal was really not such a bad arrangement for the parties concerned. True, the man probably felt slightly superior to the fair sex at this point. But as long as the woman had a post-PMS week to go somewhere to sit and relax without having to skin goats or shear sheep or make boar's head stew—did she really care? Could this law have actually been God's gift to women?

I keep picturing to myself that famous children's story where Br'er Rabbit (who'd grown up in the stickers and thickets) pleads with Br'er Bear, "Please, oh please—just don't throw me into the Brier Patch!" Only I see an Israelite woman hiding a smile as she says, "Please, oh please— you're not telling me I'm unclean, are you? What? You want me to just sit and relax, you say? I can't even lift a tiny finger to cook or clean or scrub pots or milk goats? Oy, how terrible."

Research indicates that the monthly cycles of women living together in a group (such as college dorms or in clans) tend to become synchronized until everyone is on the same schedule. Are you thinking what I'm thinking this may have meant for the women of Israel? YES! Most of the women would be ushered off—quite possibly together. Think about it: Jewish women could do Girl's Night Out, Slumber Party, Women's Retreat, or Bonko, Gobble, and Gab—all without a trace of guilt. After all, they were being put away for their "uncleanness." What could they do but stoically make the best of their dire predicament? (Of course, the Israelite men and kids were probably living it up, too—belching loudly, leaving manna crumbs and quail bones all over the tent floor.) Whatever the case, after having some time to myself to gather my thoughts, I've come to believe this "setting apart" business may be an old tradition that needs to be revisited.

In the book *Wouldn't Take Nothing for My Journey Now,* poet Maya Angelou discusses the refreshment that comes from taking some downtime for ourselves. She writes, "Every person needs to take one day away....Family, employers, and friends can exist one day without any one of us." Obviously, this was more than true for my family. They all but threw a parade to celebrate my departure.

Angelou continues, "Each person deserves a day away in which no problems are confronted, no solutions searched for. Each of us needs to withdraw from the cares which will not withdraw from us. We need hours of aimless wandering or spates of time sitting on park benches, observing the mysterious world of ants...." (I wonder if mating praying mantises—or is it manti?—count?)

"If we step away for a time," Angelou contends, "we are not, as many may think and some will accuse, being irresponsible, but rather we are preparing ourselves to more ably perform our duties and discharge our obligations."

Precisely! Doesn't a battery need to recharge? Doesn't land need time to lie fallow so that it might better nourish its crops? Caterpillars their cocooning time to better morph into butterflies? And doesn't the nurturer of the home need to be nurtured as well? I as well believe that every busy mother occasionally needs some time away in order to experience being hungry for the company of family again. Empty arms, now and again, help us appreciate how sweet two arms can feel when they are once again full of children (or husband).

✿ ✿ ✿

Well, my time here at the Wild Woman Cabin is fast coming to a close. I must shower (and shave), take the chip clip out of my hair so I can wash, roll, and brush it clean. Time to throw out the onion, brush my teeth, and chew a mint. To forage for a shirt without a tomato stain. Time to pack up the car with my books and computer, to say goodbye to the friendly forest and woodland creatures. Though I've thoroughly enjoyed my exile, I am ready for my return home. My arms are beginning to feel strangely empty. I'm also craving communication with something that's not mineral or vegetable, furred or antennaed.

Goodbye, Wild Nature Woman. I think I'm ready to prance with the poodles again.

*Very early in the morning, while it was still dark, Jesus got up, left the house and went off to a solitary place....*

MARK 1:35

A day away acts as a spring tonic.
It can dispel rancor, transform indecision,
and renew the spirit.

**Maya Angelou**

## 4

# Blowin' Up the TV

Funny thing. Though I appear on television occasionally, I have to walk over to my neighbor's house to watch my appearances—because we don't have a TV.

Well, that's not altogether accurate. We have a television, but it doesn't work except to play rented videos. (We still have a VCR.) Remember that John Denver song I loved as a teenager? The one about blowin' up the TV and movin' to the country and buildin' a home and livin' off fruit trees? There was a time I would have responded to the songwriter's lyrics by saying, "Look. We moved to the country and we're building us a home. We had a lot of children and I've given them their fair share of peaches. But if you think for one minute that I'm going to blow up the TV, well, you're off your Rockies. Erica on *All My Children* is about to reunite with husband #27 and I have to see what happens next." So God made it easy and blew up the TV for us.

Our house was literally struck by lightning, not once, not twice, but three times in one year. Blew out two modems in my computer and knocked out the television three times. After the first two incidents, we had the damaged equipment repaired, but after the third strike, we hesitated. *Could this be a sign?*

I thought about some of our friends who, several years ago, went through their own "thunder"-ous ordeal.

It happened to my friend Mary and her then husband, Gary. Within a one-month span, they went through a particularly trying time. First, Gary—a loan officer—lost his job during the height of the Texas banking industry's cutbacks. Then Mary was hit with a crippling round of mononucleosis. Their beloved Norwegian elkhound, Thor, had to be put to sleep. Finally came the crowning touch—their house was struck by lightning. It blew the phone completely off the wall, scorched a line in their living room carpet, and hit the metal pole of their carport. Leaning against that pole was their remaining dog, who ended up paralyzed in his hindquarters for several disconcerting days. His name—and I know this is hard to believe—was "Sparky." (Thankfully, Sparky had a full recovery. Until, that is, he got run over by that car....)

Mary laughs about the evening she and Gary sat around adding up all their woes and trying to make sense of the recent events. At one point Mary asked, "Gary, do you think we might be doing something wrong here?" To which Gary deadpanned, "Gee, I don't know. Would you like to ask for a sign from God?"

And they had only been struck by lightning once! We'd been hit THREE times. Sign from God or no, we stalled and didn't take the television in for repairs on its third strike out. During the first month post-TV, our family went through some pretty strange withdrawal ceremonies. We'd actually sit around the living room in our usual TV watching places, staring at the black screen as though, if we all concentrated together on the broken set, it might divinely bounce back to life just as quickly as it had been struck down.

We must have looked like a zombie support group.

The teenage boys were especially pitiful, fingering the remote control wistfully, recalling the power they once wielded in the palms of their hands.

I wandered around for two weeks in a state of suspended curiosity: "What happened with Erica and her ex-husband?" Finally, in desperation, I called a friend and asked what had transpired on the show. Nothing significant had occurred in *All My Children* Land since the television had met its demise that black and stormy night. Erica had hosted a luncheon, had bought a new dress at the boutique, and had made a couple of dramatic entrances. It was then I realized that you basically have to watch a soap opera for a good six months before the main players actually do anything. They spend four out of five weekdays dilly-dallying around with insignificant characters, repeating what they just told yesterday's insignificant characters— while we viewers put aside hugs, conversation, hobbies, work, good books, and naps and put our lives on perpetual hold. It's ridiculous when you think about it.

Eventually, the whole family started moving again in the evenings, like wooden Pinocchios coming to life. Without the TV's everpresent canned laughter and applause dominating the background, my head didn't pound any more. Without the daily bombardment of bad news, all of us grew generally more optimistic about the world we live in. Even our kids noticed it.

As I was driving a car full of teens to church one night, several of the girls began to discuss their fears of the future, of what's "out there." I brightened up when Zeke piped up from the backseat and said, "You know what? Since we haven't had a television, the world sure seems like a friendlier place."

Zeke's observation really got my brain cells firing (no easy task). I began to wonder about the wisdom of exposing the human psyche to all the evils going on in the entire world, every evening at six and ten. The news, especially, distorts reality.

And what, pray tell, IS reality?

Reality is that 70 percent of what happens each day can be seen, through grateful eyes, as a beautiful miracle.

Twenty percent, I'll grant you, is just blah and boring: brushing your teeth, trimming toenails, wiping down the kitchen counter. Ten percent of the stuff that happens is disgusting and sad and horrid and evil, and to the best of our abilities we should try to offer what relief and comfort we can to those who are hurting.

But why does the news focus on the revolting 10 percent, making us think that this is the "reality" of the world around us? It's not a true picture. It's a tiny segment chopped out of a much greater, more positive world. I cannot believe that God designed man to take in this much bad news on a regular basis. In this instance, "no news is good news" may prove to be profoundly true. It's no wonder teens often feel afraid and hopeless—even great Christian kids, who have everything to look forward to.

I know I'm ascending to dangerous soapbox territory, but I firmly believe each older generation owes its children a bright vision of their future. The "New Millennials" won't try to improve the world if we make them feel like it's a hopeless cause. I wish I could give every teenager in the country a Bible and a pair of sunglasses, with a note attached that said,

> You're about to discover in these pages that your future's so bright, you're gonna have to wear shades. So turn that boob tube off, let the Son shine in—and get out there and glow! After all, "You are the light of the world" (Matthew 5:14).
>
> With Love, from an Old Lady Who's Cheering You On

Welcome to the Freeman Family living room—five years post-television.

You'll still often find us sitting around in our old TV-watchin' spots—talking and joking with each other in the time we've recovered in our evening routines.

Usually there's a jigsaw puzzle going on the coffee table. Zach, now living on his own but not too far from home, often drops by in the evening just to chat. Zeke and his new bride pile into the living room for talking or playful newlywed wrestling about every other weekend. Gabe's working on the best physique in junior high—pumping iron or shooting baskets. Rachel's usually brushing up on her communication skills—spending her free evenings chatting on the phone or e-mailing her friends (Oh, well...). But tonight she has a gentlemen caller, and as I type this, they are sitting cross-legged on the living room floor, visiting and working on the jigsaw-puzzle-of-the-month as they eat peach cobbler (thank you, Mrs. Smith) and ice cream (and you, Blue Bell). It's ALMOST like a scene from *Leave It to Beaver,* except that I'm missing my pearls, heels, and apron.

Scott—always working on the house that will never be finished—spent the holidays up on the housetop (click-click-click) building a chimney for Good Saint Nick.

And me? Well, I haven't taken up cleaning, pumping iron, or gourmet cooking. Yet. (There's always hope.) But now I can look back over these last few years during which we finished raising our oldest two sons and let them fly away from home. And I'm grateful that when they needed to talk or wanted our attention, we never answered, "Don't interrupt, I'm watching this show" or "I'll answer you during the next commercial." Instead, when our kids and their friends dropped by and gave those telltale hints that they'd like to talk, it was usually a simple matter of putting down a hammer, looking up from a puzzle, or pouring an extra cup of coffee.

After our first year without TV, I wondered if a few years down the road, we'd be fighting over the remote control again.

But interestingly enough, it's the children who have been most insistent that we not replace the television. They simply have come to love the extra attention from us without the competition of the tube. And the number of fights between the kids at least halved when the arguments over "Turn that off! Turn that up! Switch that channel!" became moot.

We really enjoy renting videos on weekends or going out to the movies. When I'm hungry to learn something new—audibly—I love to listen to books on tape as I clean the house or take a walk. When we vacation and have access to a television, we can't believe the number of interruptions (in the form of commercials) and we usually declare it's not worth the effort to watch.

I do think there are easier ways to cut back on addictive television watching than having lightning strike your house. But our family was one of those who needed more than a gentle nudge. I'm glad God went ahead, pulled out all the stops, and zapped the TV for us. Even if it took three times before we got (or should I say lost?) the picture.

After all, the world looks much brighter since the screen went dark.

**Your lightning lit up the world.**

Psalm 77:18

# Part II

# Porch Swing Perspectives

*It's All in How
You Look at It*

## 5

# Rest on the Run

There are those times in life when naps are but a hazy memory, when chaos rains down around us so fast and so furious that we only have two options: to go nuts trying to fix the rapidly accumulating messes ourselves, or to give up and let God have the whole wacky ball of wax. Charlie Shedd shared a family story that I often think about when life gets too tangled for me to tango with. It's a story first published way back in 1962, when I was a mere babe, in a book called *Time for All Things*.

Charlie's daughter, Karen, had been working on an elaborate science experiment: an electronic model of the human brain. The project soon became too complicated for her. (I can't imagine why—how hard can it be for an elementary school kid to create a human brain? However, I guess that all depends on *whose* brain.) Anyway, she sought help from a neighboring electronic wizard named Ben.

At first Karen tried bringing over bits of the project to Ben as she finished working on each part, to get his expert input. But the project only got more confusing. One evening Karen came home, excited about a new plan she and Ben had worked out. "Ben says I should bring the whole business over to his house. Instead of me taking him the parts, he wants the whole deal. Then he'll give me the parts in their right order."

What a great concept to apply to our tangled lives!

We can just give the Master the whole deal, then let Him show us what to deal with, one thing at a time. After all, He knows where we ultimately want to be. Revealing too much at once only clogs our all-too-human brains.

One of the craziest and most chaotic weeks in my recent memory occurred a few summers ago, when I had a series of nonstop chances to put one-thing-at-a-time into practice.

It all began with a phone call from a good friend of mine, Shawn. "Becky!" she yelled into the phone. "Guess what?! I just got a call from a TV producer at ABC, the producer of the *Caryl & Marilyn Show!* You know, the show with the two real live best friends in it? They used to be on that sitcom called *The Mommies?"*

"Oh, yeah—I've seen ads for it. Looks like it's going to be a fun show."

"Well, they reminded me so much of you and me that I thought I'd write them a letter and tell them they should interview you on their show! And now Stan, one of the producers, wants to talk to you!"

"You're pullin' my leg."

"Nope. Here's his number!"

I said a hurried "goodbye and pray for me" to Shawn, then dialed the number. Before long, I found myself chatting with a real live Hollywood television producer named Stan.

"Yes, Becky!" Stan exclaimed enthusiastically. "I'm looking at your picture right here on the cover of—is it *Home Life* magazine? Anyway, I also see you've written a book called *Marriage 9-1-1*—right?"

"Well, *yes...* "

"You aren't a therapist or anything, are you?"

"No—"

"Good. Because Caryl and Marilyn aren't wild about professional know-it-all therapists."

"In that case I should be safe. I'm not a professional anything, and I don't know much."

Stan laughed, and we ended up talking for nearly an hour. He'd name a chapter title from the book and I'd give him a short blurb, or story, explaining what it was about. I guess I proved I could at least keep a conversation going because he finally said, "Okay, I'm convinced. Let's do the show! Can you fly in the day after tomorrow?"

"Sure!" I answered as I mentally zoomed by the thousand things I'd have to do in two days: make arrangements for the kids, cancel appointments, get my nails done, purchase a nice suit (I had none), and lose 20 pounds so I'd look thin in the nice suit I would buy. The deal done, all I had to do was send a fax with my bio and some questions—by the following evening—to Stan's office in Hollywood. No problem.

That is, until my temperamental computer decided to have a nervous breakdown the next afternoon—refusing to process one more word, much less tackle a fax. I'd have to hurry into town and use the fax service at the office supply store before they closed for the day. Running out the front door, papers in hand, I ran smack into my teenage son, Zeke.

"Mom!" he yelled, as I tried to brush by him in my rush to get going. "Can you give me a ride down the road so I can mow the neighbor's grass?"

"Okay," I hollered back over my shoulder, "but I've got to hurry. I've got to get a fax off to Hollywood within two hours."

"Great. And Mom—can you please, please, please let me back the station wagon out of the driveway? I'm getting really good at it and I need the practice driving."

"Zeke, this is not a good ti—"

"Please, Mom?"

"Okay, okay. But make it snappy!"

Zeke slid into the driver's seat, peered over his shoulder to make sure the coast was clear, and expertly backed the car out of the driveway—and then lodged it squarely on top of a railroad tie.

"Oh, Zeeeeeeeke!" I wailed.

"Ooops," he said. For the next 40 minutes he and I slid around on our bellies in the dirt trying to dig, pry, and cajole the car into moving. After we'd been workin' on the railroad tie what seemed like all the livelong day, a familiar man pulled up in his giant-sized pickup.

Out of the truck strolled our hero—a long, tall Texan with a Stetson, a friend of the family's named Dallas.

"Havin' some trouble, Darlin'?" he asked, sizing up our dilemma. Normally I'm not wild about being called "Darlin'," but if Big D could help me out of this fix, he could call me "Darlin'" all the livelong month. Looking for all the world like John Wayne, Dallas sauntered to the back of his pickup, pulled out the biggest jack I've ever seen (they do make things big in Texas), and in no time at all, my station wagon's wheels were back on solid ground.

"Thank you so much!" I shouted sincerely. Dallas tipped his hat and turned to leave.

"Yep, Little Darlin'," he said in parting, "now you're all undid."

This long, tall Texan had no idea how "undid" I was becoming. After dropping my teenage "back-up driver" off at his lawn-mowing job, I sped into town and faxed off the document. That accomplished, I zipped into the mall to pick up last-minute items: hose, jewelry, breath mints, a new computer. Hoping I could slide that last purchase by my husband as quickly as the salesman had talked me into buying it, I telephoned him from the mall to initiate the breaking-in process.

"Scott?"

"Yes?"

"Um, this is Becky."

"Uh-huh?"

"I just wanted to tell you that I'm on my way home. And I'll also bring home a pizza and a new computer. Do you want Dr Pepper or Coke to go with that?"

"I guess Dr Pep—you bought WHAT?!?"

"Dr Pepper it is! See you when I get home!"

I felt fairly safe in assuming Scott would not want to start a fight over a tiny, on-a-whim purchase the night before I went to my first big television debut. All my errands done, I rushed home thinking about all I still had to accomplish that evening. That old "You're Getting Be-hinder" voice was ringing in my head at full volume. There was laundry to do, and I still hadn't packed or washed my hair. I'd have to get everything done tonight because I had to leave the house by 5:30 A.M. to make it to the Dallas/Fort Worth airport in time to catch my flight. Lost in thought as I drove, I hadn't noticed the storm clouds gathering. Rain began falling in thick sheets. When I pulled up in the driveway, the rain was coming down hard and heavy, and it was completely dark outside.

Then something else caught my attention as I glanced toward the house. From the ominous looks of things, it was going to be just as dark inside as outside. Apparently the storm had knocked out our electricity (a common occurrence in these boonies). Without electricity, there would be no lights. Without lights I could not see to pack. Without electricity, there would be no washing machine or dryer—so there would be no clean laundry. Without electricity, there would be no blow dryer or curling iron—so I would look like a rain-soaked ragamuffin even if I did manage to wash my hair in the darkness.

I'd come to the place we all face at frantic times like this: Would I now run around the house screaming in panic about the unfairness of this happening before my Big Day—or would I light a candle, get in my pjs, and take Karen Shedd's advice and give the whole messy enchilada to God? Would I blow up? Or would I blow out the candle and drift off to sleep?

*Cast all your anxiety on him because he cares for you.*

1 PETER 5:7

# 6

# Hollywood, Here I Come

I walked into the dark house and grinned at the sight of Scott and the kids huddled around a lantern, playing cards. The lights in the house were off, but a light in my head had gone on.

*God,* I prayed silently, *You obviously orchestrated this opportunity. You used a handwritten letter from a friend to open a door—into Motion-Picture City, no less. So if You've turned the electricity off for now, I'm going to take it as a divine signal that I need to slow down and get some sleep. Wake me up when You are ready for me, and I'll try to take the pieces of this whole experience one step at a time. And Lord, would you mind helping Scott overlook that computer in the back seat of my car!?*

The electricity popped on around 4 A.M. It wasn't hard to tell because every appliance that had been going when the storm hit came roaring back to life. Blinding lights shone in every room, the dishwasher hummed, the microwave "pinged," the radio blared. With all this mechanical activity going on I was up, bathed, dressed, and packed for the trip in record time.

Scott escorted me to the airport, and I was grateful to note I had time to spare. When I calmly boarded the plane and found my seat, I saw, with a start, that I was going to be flying all the way to California seated next to Miss America. My seatmate had long silky brunette hair, perfect teeth, lashes a mile long—and a tiny hourglass figure tucked into a tailored red suit. She was the type of "gorgeous" that people assume happens only on movie screens. No, she wasn't really Miss America, but she certainly could have been.

*Lord, you know I really prefer to sit next to people who are bigger and uglier than me,* I started to whine, but then I remembered my promise to allow Him to order the pieces of my day. Surviving a trip next to a beauty queen was, apparently, the piece He was handing me to deal with right now.

"Hello," I said, forcing my friendliest smile.

"Hello," the Ravishing One smiled back nervously. I noticed her manicured red nails digging deep into the arms of the airplane seat. We hadn't even begun to taxi away from the gate yet.

"Nervous about flying?" I asked.

"Petrified."

"This time last year I was terrified of flying, too," I said, surprised to hear sincere sympathy in my voice, "but I had to go alone on a business trip—something I'd never done before."

"Talk to me. Keep talking," she said abruptly. "Tell me everything about it. Listening to you talk might keep from screaming and running down the aisle out the exit."

"Okaaaay," I answered slowly, being careful not to make any sudden moves. "Well, on that trip I was telling you about—I was going to Nashville and ended up sitting next to the most interesting man. An orthopedic surgeon. He even invited me to come watch him operate on a country music star's knee the next day."

"No kidding!" she exclaimed. Obviously, my distraction was working.

"And get this: We found out he and I were second cousins!"

"No!"

"Yes!"

"I mean 'No!' They're starting down the runway! I don't want to be on this airplane!"

"Everything will be fine," I said gently as I observed the panic rising in her face. Suddenly she was no longer a gorgeous model—she was a frightened little girl in need of assurance. I gently placed my hand on her arm in a gesture of sisterly comfort, looked her square in the face, and asked, "Do you believe in prayer?"

"Yes! Are you a Christian, too?!" she nearly yelled.

"Yes—and I prayed His angels would help fly our plane. I always try to image one on each wing tip—you might try that."

Once we reached cruising altitude, the color crept back into my new friend's face, and she relaxed her grip on the armrests.

"So what made you take this flight?" I asked, settling back in my seat. I was curious what would cause her to brave this experience.

"I'm on my way to a convention to be with my sister," she answered, a twinge of sadness in her voice. "She has a rare skin disorder. It distorts her face—pulls her skin tightly across her muscles—like a stretched balloon. It's very painful and even life-threatening. She used to be stunning—and now..." she paused for a moment, then continued, "well, to me she's more beautiful than ever. She's a wonderful mother, and she's been so brave through this whole ordeal. The least I could do was go with her to this medical convention. There will be lots of people there with her condition—hopefully we'll find some help."

As my new friend talked, I could see the compassion in her eyes, the love that compelled her to face her terror of flying. When I told her I was on my way to do a television interview about marriage, she opened up about the aches in her own marriage—and her lifelong battle to find self-esteem. I told her it was hard to imagine her ever battling feelings of inferiority.

"I always felt so dumb," she said. "And the truth is, I've never had a surplus of common sense."

"Oh, boy," I answered, smiling, "have you got a sympathetic ear here. I've made a whole career out of writing about the stupid things I've done."

"My husband says I'm ditzy like a fox. He thinks I'm doing all these crazy things to get attention. He just cannot comprehend how I could be such an airhead—unless I were doing it on purpose. I'm at a loss as to how to explain it to him."

So there we were: two airborne airheads—flying o'er the fruited plain (only with us aboard, it was more like flying on a fruited plane). By the time the jet landed, we'd officially bonded and had parted company promising to pray for each other's special day. I'd been taught a warm and important lesson, one I'd been needing to learn for a long time. I've often joked about it, but in truth I really have often avoided getting to know beautiful women because my self-esteem couldn't handle the contrast between their perfection and my obvious imperfections. God was showing me that hurting people come in all packages—and that I'd been holding on to what I'd assumed was a legitimate prejudice: After all, aren't all normal women allowed to be jealous of those among us who look like Barbie?

*No,* God was saying to my heart that morning, *you are not. Becky, I want you to come to the place where you see past all outward appearances and begin seeing what I see in people—their hearts.*

Once we had arrived at the airport, I looked around and found the limo driver holding up a sign with my name on it. Again I asked God to help me keep my eyes focused on the journey—especially on people and not on the "performance" ahead. Still, there were plenty of butterflies winging their way around my stomach.

The limo driver turned out to be a nice-looking guy, an aspiring screenwriter. (I was to learn that 95 percent of the people driving limos and waiting tables in Hollywood are aspiring screenwriters or actors.) He told me a little about his wife and crew of kids, then asked me about my book. I shared the CliffsNotes version of its contents. Then, when we came to a stoplight, he turned around and said, "I have a question for you: How do you know when it's time to give up on a marriage?"

"Well," I answered, "I suppose there are times when you have to let go—if the other person walks away, you can't force them to stay. But I know one thing: You shouldn't give up on a marriage just because love dies. Nearly every marriage comes to a point, somewhere along the line, where you feel like the love has died. You just have to find a way to resurrect it."

Apparently this was a radical thought in Los Angeles. I left him with a puzzled look on his face and a copy of *Marriage 9-1-1* on the front seat.

"Break a leg, Becky," the driver said kindly, as he held the door open for me while I exited the car. "I'll see you again when the show's over."

From there I was led into the Viacom Studio, smack in the middle of Sunset Boulevard. What kept surprising me about this infamous "tinsel town" was how old it was, how very—unglamorous. Though the weather was perfect, the sky had an ever present haze that put a murky damper on Hollywood's glitz. Even the studio, especially from the outside, reminded me of an aging school building. But I was greeted by the friendliest of staff assistants who did their best to put me at ease. The butterflies were settling a little.

As soon as I'd been all dolled up by the makeup artists (it's amazing, the things they can do with a little paint), I got to sneak into the studio early and watch them do a few pre-show "takes" of Caryl and Marilyn. Caryl was sitting on the kitchen set reading a book. Her job this morning was to put down the book and scream (I've now forgotten why) while stagehands pulled up on invisible strings connected to portions of her hair. The result: a "hair-raising scream." *Now THIS would be an interesting day job,* I thought to myself.

I was pleased to see how at ease Caryl and Marilyn really were—both with each other and the crew. (For those of you who remember their short-lived talk show, the friendship you saw on television is real.) Later, in the green-room, I met the other guests Stan had pulled together for today's show on "9-1-1 Emergencies." It looked to be an interesting lineup. I was there to deal humorously with marriage crises; another couple was on to share how umbilical cord blood was being used to save the lives of their children; one of the stars of the popular TV show *ER* was there to showcase her jazz singing talents—but the true star of the show was "The Cat Who Dialed 9-1-1."

I met Deputy Joe Bamford, the first officer on the cat scene, and got the real scoop straight from the source. With dark hair, quick smile, dressed in full law-enforcement regalia, Deputy Bamford was someone I liked immediately. Sure, he was a regular "Joe," but I could tell he also took his small town law duties seriously.

"Can you tell me what happened?" I asked him, feeling like a news reporter.

"Well, yes," Deputy Bamford began, his voice turning serious, with a Barney Fife edge to it. "I was on patrol when I heard the cat call come in over the radio. The victim was obviously suffering from some sort of trauma."

"How could you tell?" I asked.

"The 'me-ow, me-ows' were distressful in nature." I stifled the laugh threatening to force its way out of my mouth, as I could sense this was no laughing matter to the officer.

"I see," I managed to answer solemnly.

"Yes, well, we have to take every call seriously—you just never know. Might have been a cat, but it might have been a woman—"

"Or it might have been Cat Woman." I couldn't resist.

He continued, ignoring my comment. "The dispatcher traced the call and directed me to the location of the feline's house. I found the caller in the home, lying on the floor, flea collar lodged in its mouth. It was pulling the cat's jaw down to the proximity of its chest, causing the animal considerable discomfort. I, of course, moved to release the obstruction immediately. We later discovered that the cat had somehow landed on a telephone button that had been preset to dial 9-1-1—thereby alerting us of its predicament."

"Wow," I grinned. "Now that's a story."

"That's not even the half of it," the deputy continued. "My phone hasn't stopped ringing in two weeks. The cat, its owner, and I have been interviewed all over America, on the BBC—I even got a call from Bombay, India, the other day."

"Did you ever think you'd become famous like this?" I quizzed.

"No, my life has been pretty uneventful up to this point." For the first time in our conversation, Deputy Bamford dropped the "officer of the law" demeanor and grinned—big—like a kid who'd won a get-out-of-school pass to go play at the beach. "But I have to admit, it's really been kind of fun."

Right then the assistant producer poked her head around the corner and informed the deputy, Cat, & Company that it was time for their interview. The next hour and a half I had several delightful visits with guests, watching them leave and then viewing their segments on the video screen in the waiting area. Then came the big moment: My turn was next.

Just then Stan came around the corner looking as though he'd just heard I'd caught a fatal disease—such was the pain in his eyes. "Becky," he said, "I'm so sorry! But the show ran too long. There's no time for your segment."

*You mean I've been bumped by a CAT?* I thought, shaking my head in disbelief. These things happen only to me.

The butterflies in my stomach that had finally begun flying in formation, landed with a sickening thud. *So Lord, what's this day been about? I thought I came all this way to talk about my book on a television show and now*—I swallowed the initial disappointment and graciously thanked Stan for inviting me anyway. He turned sadly, and walked away. At that point, Caryl and Marilyn came bustling around the bend all aflutter. I smiled and shook their hands as they both began profusely apologizing at once, talking over each other just the way they do on camera. I felt like I was in the middle of a sitcom.

"Really," I interrupted, suddenly feeling more at peace about the whole thing, "it's fine. These things happen. I could have spent the day doing lots less exciting things than I got to do today. I had a great trip out here and I loved meeting you and the other guests."

At that point, Caryl dropped to her knees, took my hand, and said, "Thank you, thank you, THANK YOU for being so nice about this!"

"So some people aren't?" I asked.

The famous friends looked heavenward in disgust. "Oh, listen," said Marilyn, gesturing as she talked, "some people actually throw stuff and yell and cuss and storm out of here if they get bumped from the show."

"You're kidding?" Like synchronized swimmers, Caryl and Marilyn slowly shook their heads from left to right and back again—a silent animated answer to my question.

Just then Stan flew into our circle, his face exuberant, his hands flying. "Becky! Can you come back on Friday?"

"Well, I think so."

"Great. Listen, I want you to meet another producer—Ginger. She'll talk to you about doing Friday's show."

And that, in a nutshell, is how I ended up taking two round-trip flights to Hollywood from Dallas, Texas, in less than three days. Friday was even more fun—it was like old home week coming back to the studio. I had a ball both behind the scenes with the crew and on the segment with Caryl and Marilyn in front of a live audience (which I've always preferred to a dead one). After the show, both of the producers came backstage and invited me to come back anytime.

But back to the day I got bumped by the feline: As I walked from the studio to the waiting limo, the driver looked up and smiled. "Becky, I've got something to tell you."

"What?" I asked as he opened the door.

"Well, while you were in the studio, I've been reading your book," he leaned on the hood, then winked down at me. "I also made a phone call to my wife to tell her how much I loved her."

So why did I end up spending a whole day flying out to LA—only to end up postponed and having to do the complicated routine all over again? This was not the simple, laid-back week I'd envisioned before Shawn's phone call.

Then suddenly it was as if the Lord gave me heavenly lenses to view the scenes of the day anew.

First of all, there was a frightened woman on a plane who needed a friend. I happened to be free that day, so God worked through me to comfort one of His kids (and taught me that beauty—and fear—come in all kinds of packages). There was a limo driver who I believe needed to be encouraged—that marriage is tough, but it's worth the work to keep it.

Then there was me, the hurried woman who needed to see how faithful God is to bless our days and to use us as His vessels when we let Him lead us one step at a time. Little by little, He's showing me I can rest on the run. And that people are more important than our destination. For human connections are a huge part of the jubilees we'll enjoy on life's journey. Then, too, I've a feeling God knew I'd get a royal kick out of meeting The Cat Who Dialed 9-1-1.

(Not to mention...it gave an anonymous, impulsive woman an opportunity to be 3000 miles away from her husband when he discovered the price tag on that new computer in the backseat of the car.)

✿ ✿ ✿

*If I go up to the heavens, you are there....If I settle on the far side of the sea, even there your hand will guide me.*

PSALM 139:8-10

# 7

# Botchin' It, Big Time

**E**ver had one of those times when you felt like you made a mess of everything you touched?

Me too. (In fact, Scott laughs over the realization that I've actually made a career out of reporting on all the messing up I do.)

One particularly vivid messup began innocently, on a Monday night in spring when I agreed to do something totally out of my league, light-years removed from my natural talents. If I'm honest with myself, this may be partly why I agreed to do it. It's hard for me to dodge a challenge. Besides, as you know, I believe God likes using the most unlikely people to accomplish His purposes (His basic M.O. being to confound the wise, one fool at a time). It keeps everybody on his toes and slightly amazed.

A friend of mine, motivational speaker Suzie Humphreys (featured in my book *Real Magnolias*), is famous for saying, "Volunteer! You can learn it later." Only now I've added my own motto to hang up alongside Suzie's: "Volunteer! If you blow it badly, next time you could be told that the best thing you can do to 'help the cause' is stay home and take care of yourself." Either way, you win.

Anyway, on the particular Monday under discussion, a parachurch organization called Young Life was hosting a fund-raising banquet. (Aside: Does the word "parachurch" make anybody else picture a steepled building dangling from a parachute? My mind works like this all the time, but I've discovered that it can frighten people, so I mostly keep it to myself.) Anyway, the Sunday before the banquet a pair-a-leaders cornered me at church and said, "Hey, Becky, we've got a favor to ask. We need someone to give the financial pitch—the close—at our fund-raising banquet. It's the most important part of the evening, really. But it should be very simple, just a three-to-five-minute deal. We think you'd be perfect."

I raised one eyebrow suspiciously. "Financial pitch? You do know that I think balancing my checkbook means keeping it level so it won't fall out of my purse, don't you? I'm not exactly what you'd call a financial wizard. I'm probably not even what you could call a financial munchkin."

"That's okay. Really, this won't be a big deal, and you'll be helping a tremendous ministry reach out to high school kids."

"Ooooh. I get it. You couldn't get anyone else to do this, so you're asking me, right?"

"Right."

"Okay, that makes me feel much better. Your expectations can't be all that high, then. What do I do?"

"Why don't we meet tomorrow for breakfast and we'll brief you?"

"Right," I answered. Then, wanting to add a touch of business savvy, I added, "And I'll try to bring some briefs for you, too."

They gave each other a puzzled look, and I walked away wondering if these folks had any idea what they were taking on. But if they were brave enough to ask, I was willing to give being an overnight financier my best shot.

The Official Briefing took place at the International House of Pancakes—because Jim, the main leader, had some great coupons. Jim and his wife, Terry, got right down to business, doing an admirable job of outlining the resources and challenges of the ministry on the back of a menu, but bless their hearts, they had no way of knowing how morning-impaired I am. The main thought on my mind as I struggled to focus on the scribbled figures was, *Where's that cheery blue-aproned waitress with the big pot of coffee anyway? If somebody will give me caffeine IMMEDIATELY, I might not conk out on this little plate of butter pats.*

To further add to my distraction, one of the Young Life assistant leaders, Kelly, had come along for the ride (and the Buy-One-Get-One-Free Breakfast Coupon). This is a good place to mention that a qualification for working with a high school ministry is that one must be skilled at performing a great variety of silly kid tricks. This morning, Kelly was in rare form.

The coffee had finally come, and I was slowly coming to life. Jim and Terry and I were busily chatting as Kelly, who was sitting next to me, began nonchalantly peeling the pulp out of a lemon slice. Then—unseen by me—he cut a few strategic slits in the peel, turned it inside out so the white part was showing, and positioned the wedge between his front teeth and upper lip. When I happened to glance to my left, Kelly nearly startled me out of the booth with what appeared to be the biggest set of buckteeth I'd ever laid eyes on. Under the best of circumstances it's hard for me to concentrate on economics and finances. But now that a semigrown man with a huge citrus overbite had entered our conversation—my mind lost any shred of pertinent information Jim and Terry had imparted thus far.

*Not to worry,* I told myself. *Haven't I just been invited to that banker's convention? Shouldn't that count toward some measure of monetary adeptness?*

I assured Jim and Terry that I had the gist of the idea and that all would be fine.

"After all, guys," I asked with a laugh, "how can I mess up a three-minute talk? Besides, I'm getting more and more comfortable in front of groups these days. Just make me a couple of transparencies with all the vital facts and numbers. We can meet before the banquet and run over the figures once more before I get up to speak. The overhead will be a big help."

That evening I arrived early at the Community Center (where the banquet was being held) and saw that the Young Life crew was already in full swing. Poor Jim was so busy putting out fires, coordinating caterers, and practicing with the music and drama team that I could see we were going to have to pitch the idea of practicing the pitch.

*It'll be fine,* I soothed myself once again. *If I'm anything, I'm a professional.* Somewhere another voice in my head shot back, *Yeah, but a professional WHAT?* Tonight I prayed fervently that I would come off as a professional pitcher. A professional financial pitcher, that is.

The guests arrived, and we all sat down at paper-covered metal tables to eat our paper-tasting banquet food from stiff paper plates. Somehow during the dinner I managed to drop a piece of strawberry cake on a transparency Jim had hurriedly given me before the guests started pouring in. I wiped at the smear with my napkin, thinking it really wasn't all that noticeable. It was then, for the first time, that I got a good look at what was to be my visual aid. It was a page of tiny numbers arranged in columns. I panicked as I realized I had no idea what any of them meant, or what a ditzy girl like me was doing in a place like this. But it was too late—the show had to go on.

The Young Life gang did a marvelous job: The skits were hilarious, the songs were upbeat and inspiring, and the main speaker delivered one of the most touching messages I'd ever heard on God's unconditional love! Now all I had to do was close us out. Tie up the bow. Give the invitation to make Greenville's Young Life dreams a firm reality.

On my way up to the podium I tripped on the stage. When I got to the microphone, it was towering above me like an awkward giraffe. I could not figure out how to lower it, so I bent the flexible metal neck into sort of an upside-down "U" shape and talked up into the mic itself. "There," I said, and my own voice, echoing louder than I had anticipated, made me jump. Realizing I could not spend the whole evening with my neck straining up like a small child trying to reach a water fountain, I patted the microphone contraption into more of an "S" and finished my sentence: "There now. Here we go."

I began by sharing a heartfelt testimony of what Young Life had meant to me as a teenager, piggybacking on the wonderful message that had just been given. So far so good. But then the time came where I had to turn on the overhead to display the transparency on the screen and explain the ministry's current financial situation and pro-jected needs. Do you know how HUGE an otherwise inconspicuous cake smear looks when it is projected onto a banquet-hall wall? Believe me, a six-foot cake smear is something to be reckoned with. There was nothing I could do but try to explain its presence.

Things began going downhill from there, with me stam-mering and pitifully trying to explain what those little fig-ures meant, tossing out financial-sounding phrases I'd heard as I went along. Mutual Fun. Crediting Debits. It was not convincing. Imagine Lucy Ricardo from one of the classic "I want to be in Ricky's act" episodes; one of those shows where Lucy thinks she can ballet with the best of 'em only to realize, too late, that she's in over her head and her only hope now is to escape, leaving as little damage behind as possible.

"This is just the sort of disaster that can happen," my Eeyore-like husband often warns, "to overoptimistic people."

Actually, if I had to pick an old television icon that best described how I sounded by the time I got to the smeared overhead, it would probably be Mary Tyler Moore's character from the old *Dick Van Dyke Show*. Remember how Laura's voice would quiver when she had to explain why she was in such a bind?

I remember saying, "Well, um, I think what this, um, basically means...is that, um, i-i-if you have, say, a whole lot of money, well, um, y-you should—probably, I mean I think—you should give a whole l-l-lot of money. And i-i-if you don't have very much money, th-then you should put some quarters in a F-Folger's can and save it until y-you have a bunch. I th-think. 'Ooooh, R-r-r-o-o-b!'"

Only I didn't call for Rob, I called for Jim—who had very much wanted to stay out of the financial appeal limelight this evening. He tried his best to save me, but in the end we just did our best to sort of patch up and close out the night. However, I did a really professional job, I must say, of explaining how to tear off the "commitment section" from the brochure, drawing on my experience as a first-grade teacher. I'm not sure, but I think I also closed us in prayer. I know I prayed for it all to come to a close!

Afterward, I found Scott's arms and fell into them laughing and crying at the same time. Somewhere behind me I heard a woman say, "She's so cute." And another several women said, "That's exactly the kind of financial explanation I've always wanted to hear at these things." But this was one time I really didn't want to be cute. I wanted to be savvy. Or smooth. Or spiritual. Anything but silly. Too much was at stake.

Once we got home, Scott, my reserved husband (who almost never laughs out loud), fell onto the bed in a fit of hysterics. Wouldn't you know it would be my disaster that tickled his funny bone. "Oh, Becky, that was SOOO awful! Do you know how awful that was? I mean (hee-hee) it was so awful that it was the most hilarious thing I've ever seen. It was like a skit from *Saturday Night Live* or something."

I started to cry and through my tears said, "But I didn't mean to be funny this time! This was serious. An important ministry is in the balance here!"—but then I found myself laughing hysterically along with Scott, through my tears. Just about the time we'd both stop laughing and rolling on the floor, Scott would come up for air and repeat, "Oh, that was just AWFUL," and we'd be off holding our stomachs and laughing again. When I finally calmed down, I called Jim's answering machine and left a lengthy message of apology for my first, and last, speech on the economics of ministry.

For the next few days after my nosedive, I received a series of notes and phone calls that were very interesting. They were meant to be thank-you notes and "we appreciate your participation" phone calls, but invariably they all ended up sounding more like humorous sympathy cards. Jim's consolation at church the following week was only semi-comforting.

"Becky," he said, patting me on the back, "now I don't want you to worry about it one more minute. Do you really think you could have said or done anything that could undo that great message the other speaker gave?" I smiled and nodded while inside I thought, *Wow. I was THAT bad?* Reading between the lines, I interpreted Jim to mean, "Becky, just make sure that whenever you speak in public, the speaker before you is SO good that no matter what you do or say, they will only remember Speaker #1." And for some reason this was just not making me feel better.

✿　✿　✿

The day after Jim's comment, I was traveling down an exit ramp off Interstate 30 when I witnessed a two-car collision. It looked as though the drivers were okay, but there was some serious fender-bending. Wanting to be a good citizen (actually wanting to be a good at just something—ANYTHING), I pulled off at the next convenience store and dialed 9-1-1. The operator picked up.

"Yes, operator," I said breathlessly into the pay-phone receiver, "I just witnessed a small wreck on the exit ramp...." I poured it all out at once—the location, a detailed description of the vehicles involved, extent of injuries, my name and home number. Finally, when I ran out of steam, the operator spoke up.

"Ma'am?"

"Yes?"

"What number did you dial?"

"9-1-1!"

"I'm sorry. You dialed 4-1-1. This is Information, may I connect you to 9-1-1?"

*That does it,* I thought. *Is this "Becky Fails at Everything" Week?* I'd seen news stories where toddlers in DIAPERS saved the day by dialing 9-1-1. I'd been formally introduced to a CAT that found a way to paw 9-1-1! Three little numbers was all I had to remember. I had even botched being a good citizen.

✿　✿　✿

The next awful thing I did that very same week involved Kelly (the guy with the lemon-peel teeth), a prized book, and a Nutty Airline Company. Rather than go into detail, I'll just let you read an excerpt of the following letter, faxed in desperation to Herb Kelleher, CEO of Southwest Airlines:

> Southwest Airlines Co.
> Chairman of the Board
> Herb Kelleher
> President & Chief Executive Officer
> Love Field
> Dallas, Texas
>
> Dear Herb:
>
> Help!!!!!!!!
>
> Let me back up. Southwest has an employee, a flight attendant named Kelly Gaudreau, who was president of his graduating class. There could not be a more enthusiastic cheerleader for you and Southwest than Kelly. Not long ago, my son and I ran into Kelly at a restaurant, and he insisted that we come over afterwards so he could give us an airplane model and show me a special Southwest employee video and show me his cherished copy of your new book, *Nuts!*—a special edition personally signed by you and your assistant, Colleen.
>
> Well, I'm a humorous writer and speaker (I have to do something with all the disasters I get myself into), and I often open my talks saying, "I come from a long line of nuts..." Sure enough, I opened the back of your book and found my Uncle James listed there. He was the arm-wrestling champion of the state of Texas (the 61-year-old guy) who took your

place at the famous Malice in Dallas event. *Great,* I thought, *this would be a cute fact to toss into my opening.*

So I asked Kelly if I could borrow his book, promising to take extra good care of it (I even took the dust jacket off so it wouldn't get creased).

Then today, I looked outside at the porch swing where I usually read and yelled, "NOOO—oh, God, please NO!" Because there all soaked and bleeding and ruffled from last night's rain storm was Kelly's prized possession—his *Nuts!*—gone.

It is at this point that I'd like to begin my official begging for a special dispensation and ask you to sign another copy of a book (if I buy it and bring it to your office? on my knees?) that I can give to Kelly. I just can't face him with this.

Look, Herb, you seem like a nice guy. And I'm just having an all-round bad week.

Please, please, oh, pretty, pretty please sign a copy of *Nuts!* for Kelly to replace the one I ruined and you'll have a fan for life. I'm an author too. (Though not a CEO of an airline or anything. Actually I'm not even a real good airline passenger.) I know what a hassle this signing thing can be, but there are special cases...and believe me, this qualifies.

Love and Laughter (with fingers crossed),

Becky Freeman

Now if you were Herb, wouldn't you have had pity on me? Unfortunately, according to the Polite and Professional Public Relations Person at Southwest, they are all out of the special edition copies, and Herb isn't signing any more. Even most of the employees didn't get one. (If he signs one, he has to sign thousands.) "But," she said perkily, "we so enjoyed your humorous letter."

*Look,* I felt like shouting, *I don't want applause here for writing a cute letter. I want mercy!! I want a new book and I want it signed by Herb. H-e-r-b. Four little letters. How hard can that be???*

Ah, well. I guess this is just one of those cases where my stupidity and lack of planning does not constitute an emergency for a busy airline president. (Herb, if you're reading this, I still think you are a nice guy. And I understand policy is policy. But let's face it—you really missed a chance to come out the hero in this chapter.)

By the end of this week, I was NOT feeling good about myself.

### The End

*What??* you say. *That's all? That's the end? Where's the sunny little saying, the silver lining, the happy story that suddenly makes you feel on top of the world again? Where's the tie-it-all-up-in-a-neat-bow porch-swing epiphany?*

Sorry. The only porch swing scene in THIS chapter is the one where I discovered that big, ruffled, soaked *Nuts!* book. But being familiar with human nature, I know that sometimes the best thing we can say to each other to cheer ourselves up is, "Man, did I ever blow it—BIG TIME—this week." Now, you see, you can compare your week to mine and close the book right here feeling infinitely better about yourself. Be my guest.

Actually, something did happen near the end of this week that helped me put my life back in perspective. It involved my youngest son.

And a gun.

(On second thought, maybe you shouldn't close the book yet.)

*My soul is downcast within me; therefore I will remember you.*

PSALM 42:6

## 8

# Relaxing with Our Flaws

I was washing dishes at the kitchen sink when suddenly I heard something hit glass. Whirling around, I saw one tiny round hole in our living room window, then watched in disbelief as the huge eight-by-four-foot window cracked into a thousand pieces. Through this odd mosaic of glass, I saw that Gabe had fallen to the ground outside.

I was rushing out the door when suddenly he stood up, stared at the window in shock, threw his BB gun down on the ground, and ran around the house holding his hands over his eyes—as if by doing so he could shut out what had happened. I found him several minutes later on his big brother's bed, his whole body buried under the covers, convulsed with sobs.

"Gabe, Gabe," I said soothingly as I sat down near the lump on the bed, "it's going to be okay. Are you all right?"

"No!" he shouted, never one to stuff his feelings. Between sobs, from under the covers he cried, "I tripped and the gun fired up instead of down. I want to be invisible! I want to be in another country. I don't know what to do. I can't face Daddy! He just finished building that pretty room! Will you take me somewhere far away?? I can live somewhere else!!"

"Oh, Gabe," I said, holding his mummified-in-blankets form and rubbing what I guessed to be his back, "accidents happen. All of us blow it sometimes. Think of all the stupid things I did this week. Remember how I left that important book out in the rain? And just last week, your daddy slammed into the front door with his back, trying to move in a piece of equipment, and he shattered the glass in it! Daddy won't be upset—he knows how bad you feel already. I'll go get him and explain what happened. You'll see what I mean."

I left to find Scott and plead Gabe's case. I quickly informed him of the mishap, and within minutes Scott had taken my place as Comforter there on the bed beside his grieving son. As I passed by the bedroom, I saw Scott holding Gabe in his arms, stroking his dark hair, telling stories of all the baseballs he'd thrown through windows when he was a kid.

"Son, it's just something ten-year-old boys do at least once in their lives. You'll be more careful from now on. We're just glad you aren't hurt. Glass can be replaced, people can't." Gabe fell asleep within minutes, totally exhausted from his ordeal of self-flagellation.

Observing Gabe's trauma I wondered, *Have I really changed all that much since I was a child? When it comes to making mistakes, aren't I more like a ten-year-old than I want to admit—punishing myself mentally over and over again for not being perfect?* And all along, my Father is there beside me holding out comfort, saying, "Becky, did you forget again? You don't have to be perfect. You don't even have to be all that good at anything. Just be yourself. I forgave you long ago, so forgive yourself—and let me rock you and hold you and love you when you blow it. Then get back up and go after it again. I'll be here whenever you need me."

Charles Spurgeon, who battled depression and low moods, said, "The strong are not always vigorous, the wise not always ready, the brave not always courageous, and the joyous not always happy." We can't let our mistakes or temporary down times or even our lapses into sin define who we really are. We may be acting weak, depressed, and immature, but who we are is what God sees. Because what God sees, when He looks at our hearts, is Jesus.

Do you ever get into one of those head-hanging, "please-don't-hit-me" attitudes toward God? It's that generalized feeling that says, "I'm not measuring up to His standards, so He's probably mad at me, or at the very least, He wants something from me—but I don't know what it is." I once read something by C.S. Lewis that his wife had related to him, a story that I found enormously comforting for times like this. So comforting, in fact, that I typed it out and filed it under "Thoughts That Make My Neck Muscles Unwind."

Lewis wrote,

> Joy tells me that once, years ago, she was haunted one morning by a feeling that God wanted something of her, a persistent pressure like the nag of a neglected duty, and till midmorning she kept on wondering what it was. But the moment she stopped worrying, the answer came through as plain as a spoken voice. It was, "I don't want you to do anything. I want to give you something," and immediately her heart was full of peace and delight.

Have you ever watched a toddler in a desperate struggle to put toothpaste—that he's just squirted all over the bathroom—back into the tube? How vividly I remember quietly watching my child from the doorway, chuckling to myself, waiting for him to turn his helpless chubby hands up to me and offer an "uh-oh" grin in my direction. I believe our heavenly Father also often shakes His head and sometimes even smiles as we struggle to fix the unfixable by ourselves. He patiently waits until we've exhausted ourselves and finally offer the mess we've made of our lives up to Him.

Waits for us to poke our heads out of the covers long enough to let Him render aid and comfort.

He doesn't want anything from you.

He wants to give something to you: the compassion of a Dad who understands we are kids made of all-too-human clay.

*The Lord is compassionate and gracious, slow to anger, abounding in love....As a father has compassion on his children, so the Lord has compassion on those who fear him.*

Psalm 103:8,13

# I'm Flawed, Therefore I Am

My sister Rachel and I have burned up the phone line between us this past year as we've shared our struggles to give up "performing," and we're finding new contentment in simply relaxing as daughters of a loving Father. Our midlife battles have included overcoming disillusionment with God, motherhood, marriage, our shortcomings, and life in general.

Now, as we are both coming out of our own tunnels, we're catching brilliant glimpses of light—light that comes from accepting ourselves, flawed as we are, and clinging to the reality of God's grace. And we are also discovering that flaws, unlike sins, are really imperfections that God has carved out of our lives—like scoops in puzzle pieces—where other people can fit in and feel needed!

Recently, Rachel sent me a page from a book called *The Joy of Imperfection*. I smiled at the list of affirmations placed at the end of one of the chapters:

- I fondly accept my imperfections.

- I have fabulous flaws.

- My flaws make me unique and therefore priceless.

- Love me; love my flaws.

- I am greater than any one part of me.

- I'm always a partial success.

- I'm totally lovable, even though he, she, or they don't love me.

- I'm flawed, therefore I am.

Relax. God made us—flaws and all. He's not out to get us. On the contrary, He's out to give us something: the unconditional love of a parent for a child—even a child who messes up a lot.

# 9

# WORMS of the World, Unite!

**M**any authors these days have symbols of their own unique personalities. When we think of Barbara Johnson, we visualize geraniums in broad-rimmed hats. When we picture Chuck Swindoll, a Harley-Davidson roars to mind. When *Worms in My Tea* first appeared in bookstores, I never dreamed my name would forever be intertwined with a slimy invertebrate.

To make matters worse, in the publishing world a book's title is most often given a nickname to simplify communication. While I was touring my publishing company for the first time, an eager young woman introduced me to a group of salespeople by proudly announcing, "This is Becky Freeman—she's our author with *Worms.*" (Don't you know how eager they were to shake hands with me after that intro?) Since that happening, I've played around with the idea of changing my business card to read:

### Becky Freeman

*"The Author with Worms"*

Or better yet, I've thought about using the name "WORMS" as an acronym for my own organization. But what would I want the acronym to stand for? (Not to mention who or what could I possibly organize?) This morning I found myself shouting "I've got it!" as I was struck with inspiration. May I present the name of my proposed organization:

## WORMS, INC.

### Women Overcoming Ridiculous, Mind-boggling Situations

This says it all. Because I've accepted that my life's purpose and mission is to encourage like-minded women who are struggling to overcome the ridiculous and mind-boggling situations life throws our way—through my writing and speaking and driving into muddy ditches. I looked up the word "ridiculous" in my thesaurus this morning and found the following listed: "absurd, ludicrous, preposterous, nonsensical, foolish, silly, idiotic, irrational, unreasonable, senseless, outlandish; laughable, comical, funny, droll, amusing; farcical, crazy." When I showed this to Scott, he asked, "Are you sure you're not looking up the word 'Becky'?"

"No," I answered indignantly, "my name is closer to 'mind-boggling,' which means 'extraordinary, phenomenal, remarkable, amazing, incredible, astounding, indescribable'—and my personal favorite—'stunning.'"

He managed a weak smile, the sort of smile he usually saves for surprise visits from unwanted callers.

But I stunningly ignored him.

To assume the leadership of such a prestigious organization as WORMS, Inc., one must of course have the necessary qualifications and experience. Besides the volumes I've already written, I'd like to submit the following story of how I persevered in overcoming a recent series of ridiculous, mind-boggling circumstances. It should demonstrate why I'm most qualified to pilot WORMS.

Our family was visiting Scott's parents in Azle (about a two-hour drive from us) this past Thanksgiving. Scott and the children decided to stay over for an extra day, but I needed to get back home to work on a writing assignment. Since we had driven two cars, I drove home alone, leaving late that evening, so I could get an early start the next morning. On the drive home, I went the wrong direction several times because it was dark and, well, you know how different the world looks when the lights are off. But I overcame this adversity by driving through several all-night fast-food places until I finally happened upon a teenager with sufficient wits to point me in the right direction.

When I arrived at the gate to the entrance of our little lakeside community, it was around 2 A.M., and I found myself in the first of a series of mind-boggling predicaments. I hadn't remembered to get a key to the gate from Scott. I contemplated turning away and driving to a motel, but thought, *No, that would be silly. Our house is only a mile down the road there beyond this locked gate. Surely I can figure out a way to get around the gate and to the house.* Then I remembered a roundabout, back-road entrance the kids had once shown me. All I'd have to do is drive through a pasture, around some ponds and trees, and over and up a couple of hills.

I turned the wheels of my little Subaru and headed toward the pasture. I got maybe 100 yards before I realized I was driving in grass-camouflaged mud. And with the sun long since gone to bed, I could not tell whether the dark thing now looming in front of me was a hill, a pond, or a tree. None of the three possibilities would be good news. So praying hard, I carefully backed out—slipping and sliding, but never getting stuck—and landed right back at my starting place. At least my Subaru and I were not wound around a tree or at the bottom of a fish pond, but still there was the locked gate to contend with.

More determined than ever to get home alone, I parked on the side of the road, took my purse, locked the doors to my car, and walked up to the seven-foot-high gate. Tossing my purse over the top, I waited until I heard it land with a thud on the other side Then I began my ascent. A middle-aged woman doesn't get many chances to climb fences, and I actually thought it rather fun. Like being in the third grade again. Of course, I'd rather have enjoyed this jaunty climb on a sunny day than on a cold, misty night at 3 A.M.—but we overcomers must look on the bright side, mustn't we?

I picked up my purse from the asphalt, resolutely slinging it over my shoulder, and began the mile-long trek to our home. Have I mentioned yet how dark it was? In the country, there are no boosts of illumination from nearby city lights. I felt like Snow White, walking through shadowy cartoon forests—the trees taking on a dark life of their own on either side of the road. The hoot owls once gave me such a start that I jumped and dropped my purse and had to grope for it on the ground like a blind woman.

I kept repeating comforting things from the Bible I'd learned as a child: *At times I am afraid I will trust in Thee. You are a very present help in times of trouble.* Before long, my heart stopped pounding, and I was actually beginning to enjoy the quiet night and the stars overhead. Until my new boots rubbed two fresh blisters into the sides of my tender feet. I was also beginning to feel the painful effects of having downed a super-sized cola on the drive home.

Finally, thankfully, I made my way to my front door and nearly fell on the welcoming front porch with gratitude. "Ah, Home Sweet Home," I said, leaning against the door to open it. But something was awry with my home sweet home. The door was locked. Now I realize that for most people this is not unusual. Most folks lock the front doors of their houses when they go away for any length of time. But since we had left only for the day and Scott knew I'd be coming home alone, a locked door raised all sorts of dire suspicions. Then I realized something else: The dogs weren't barking. Daisy, our Brittany spaniel, and Colonel, the little schnauzer,

ALWAYS bark either in greeting to us or in warning to strangers. Something was terribly wrong with this picture—besides the fact that the door was locked and I was, once again, keyless (not to mention clueless).

Burglars, obviously, had killed the dogs and locked me out of my own house. I hate it when that happens. But "WORMS shall overcome" is my motto, so I did not give up. I would go find help.

However, where does one go for help, on foot, at 3:35 A.M.? My feet bleeding, my head pounding, my bladder aching, I grabbed up my purse and marched toward our neighbors, Melissa and Michael Gantt. Yes! I brightened when I saw their car in the driveway. At least they were in town. I hated to wake them up at this hour, but felt, for my own safety, I had to get someone to help me find a way into my house and lend comfort should I need to grieve the loss of my pets and all my worldly possessions.

I knocked. And knocked. And knocked and knocked. Not a creature would stir in my neighbor's house. I turned the knob, and to my surprise the front door popped open.

"Melissa!" I yelled.

Nothing.

"Michael!" I hollered. Still all was quiet. *Oh, great,* I thought, *maybe the burglar got Michael and Melissa too.* So I walked into the darkened kitchen, noticed a phone because of its glowing buttons, picked it up, and dialed Scott's parents' home.

"Beverly?" I asked when my mother-in-law answered the phone on its second ring.

"Yes?"

"I'm so sorry for calling this late. Or this early. I guess it's morning, isn't it? Can I please speak to Scott? I've broken into my neighbor's house and I'm using their phone because I can't break into our house."

"What?"

"It's a long story. Could I just speak with Scott?"

"Sure," she answered and in a few seconds, Scott was on the phone.

"Becky?" he asked sleepily.

"Yes?"

"Why am I talking to you on the phone at four in the morning?"

"Well, Scott..." and I explained what had happened up to that point. "So you see," I continued, "I'm worried because the doors are locked and the dogs are probably dead. And I'm in someone else's house without their knowledge, using their phone to talk to you. And they may be dead, too, but I'm too afraid to go look and see."

"Don't you dare, Becky!" Scott objected. "You're lucky Michael hasn't woken up and shot you, thinking you are an intruder."

"I am an intruder, just a friendly one."

"But they don't know that!"

"What should I do?" I lowered my voice to a whisper.

"Go home. I locked the doors this morning and forgot to tell you. The dogs are probably over at George's house down the street. You know how they love to go over there when we're gone—he's always feeding them treats and letting them in for a visit."

"How will I get in?"

"Climb through the side window."

"Gotcha. See ya tomorrow—if I'm alive and all."

"You'll be fine."

I gently put the phone down, wondered if I should risk using the Gantt's bathroom before I left, decided my bladder would have to tough it out, and tiptoed back out of the front door, forcing my aching feet back to my own home. I had to get a ladder to reach the unlocked window, but once inside I nearly kissed the linoleum. The dogs were nowhere to be seen, but the house was exactly as we had left it: completely ransacked.

I breathed a sigh of relief, ran to the bathroom to take care of my most pressing need, then took a hot bath, put Band-Aids on my blisters, and fell into bed. Scott called just to make sure I hadn't killed myself climbing through the window. I assured him I was fine and that if there were burglars hiding in the house, I no longer cared—as long as they went about their work quietly and let me sleep. *All is well,* I thought as I finally fell into a deep slumber. *You, Lord, only make me dwell in safety. Thank you for taking care of me. Together, we have overcome.*

I'd been asleep a full hour when the phone rang. I checked the red digital numbers on the alarm clock: 5:30 A.M. Picking up the phone, I wearily answered, "Hello?"

"Becky?" the voice on the other end sounded concerned.

"Yes?"

"This is Janet—I live near the gate."

"Yes, Janet, what's up?"

"Well, I'm sorry to call so early, but the paperboy came by this morning and gave me a credit card belonging to you. Said he'd found it on the ground near the gate."

I explained what had transpired the night before, and Janet offered to pick me up, take me to the gate, and open it with her key. I accepted her offer—this way I could also get my car off the road and check for any more credit cards that might have fallen out of my purse when I threw it over the gate. When I got to the gate—sure enough—I found another credit card sticking out of a pile of leaves. I thanked Janet for her help and told her to pass on my gratitude to the paperboy, then drove back home.

*You know, I'd better check my purse to see if there are any more cards missing,* I thought before I dropped back into bed. But now my purse was nowhere to be found. I looked everywhere I could possibly have left it. "I can't believe this!" I yelled aloud to an empty house. Then I realized what had probably happened. I must have left my purse outside the window when I crawled into the house. A burglar must have seen it there in the porchlight and stolen it!

I dialed the sheriff's office. It was now 6:15 A.M., and I'd had more activity throughout the night than I get in most days. When the dispatcher picked up the phone I said, "Yes, this is Becky Freeman. I just wanted to report a stolen purse, in case you recover any of my checks or credit cards or anything."

"And where was your purse stolen?"

"It was stolen where I left it outside last night when I crawled through the window to get into my house." I went on to explain, as best as I could, the events of the night and my personal theory on my purse's disappearance. The dispatcher seemed anxious to get off the phone, but wished me the best in locating the purse snatcher.

*I'd better call up to the Village Market too,* I thought, *just in case someone tries to cash one of my checks there. It's the closest place for a burglar to try to pull something like that.* Melissa answered the phone. (Michael and Melissa are not only our neighbors and friends, they also own the Village Market.)

"Hello, Gantt's Village Market, can I help you?"

"Melissa?

"Becky?"

"Melissa! You're not dead!"

"No," she sounded confused, "but I feel like it. I had to open the store this morning and Michael and I had both taken antihistamines last night for our colds. I'm still having a hard time keeping my eyes open." *So that explained their sound sleeping!*

"Becky?" Melissa's voice, sounding both curious and perplexed, interrupted my thoughts.

"Yes?"

"The weirdest thing happened—we found your purse in our kitchen this morning."

How embarrassing. I explained my breaking and entering to Melissa, who immediately hollered for Michael to "come hear what Becky's done now."

Then I dialed the sheriff's department.

"Please don't worry anymore about my missing purse," I explained jubilantly. "I found it! I left it in the other house I broke into last night! Isn't that wonderful?"

The dispatcher agreed that it was and quickly hung up the phone.

Relieved to have located my purse and completely exhausted, I fell back into bed and into a deep sleep—for an entire 30 minutes—before the phone rang again. 7 A.M. Still a mite early to be getting calls on a weekend morning. I picked up the phone and recognized the sweet voice of another friend and neighbor, Wally. (Out in the country, most neighbors are friendly.)

"Becky?" There was something oddly familiar about the way this conversation was starting.

"Yes?"

"Becky, I was jogging this morning, and about halfway between the gate and your house, I found three of your credit cards!"

"Oh, Wally, thank you! I must have dropped them out of my purse when that owl hooted." Then I went through the entire story again with Wally, who sounded even more confused by the time I'd finished. I had to admit, the saga was getting more complicated with every phone call.

The next day, my son found the last missing credit card on the road while riding his bike. In those wee morning hours I'd apparently been like Gretel of fairy tale fame— only, instead of dropping crumbs, I'd been dropping credit cards to mark my path.

I am so blessed to have friends and neighbors who are honest and caring. The kind who understand when you get locked out at the gate and have to climb over it and walk home at three o'clock in the morning. And when you can't get in, they understand when you break into their house and leave your purse but you don't know it so you have to call the sheriff and report it stolen and then when you find out it wasn't, you have to call back and retract the report. They understand when you have to crawl through the window of your own house because you have no keys to anything whatsoever and when you leave credit cards strewn over a mile-long length of road.

Well, maybe they don't understand. But they do try to be supportive in my struggle to be a WORM: a Woman Over-coming yet another string of Ridiculous, Mind-boggling Situations.

And so, WORMS of the world—wriggle out to the porch and relax. Not only is there now a support group for us, but we can hold our heads up out of the dirt with pride as we realize anew our purpose on earth: to give the rest of the world a chance to pause, scratch their heads, and ask, "WHAT?"

### *God provided a worm...*

JONAH 4:7

# Part III

# A Little Less Laundry, a Lot More Fun

*Choosing to Nourish
Your Emotional Life*

## 10

# In Search of Joy Triggers

There's an old Chinese saying I love: "After ecstasy, the laundry."

Isn't that the truth? There's a time for ecstatic, incredible, magnificent experiences—and then, there's a time for pouring detergent into a tub full of dirty socks. Funny how we seem to need both so we can stay balanced in our porch swings of life.

Our second son, Zeke, is affectionately known as the "sweet, spiritual" one in our family. That is, he's been blessed with a tender heart, a peace-loving nature, and an insatiable curiosity about the things of God. He's always lived for adventure—constantly planning and executing huge events through his high school years, like evangelistic outdoor concerts or backpacking/rock-climbing/water-rafting/parachuting/bungee-jumping class field trips.

Zeke's the kind of guy who revels in life's ecstatic, mountaintop moments. So it's been tough, sometimes, when Scott and I have had to remind this wonder child that there's a pile of laundry waiting at the bottom of Thrill Hill.

I remember one morning in particular, when Scott needed Zeke to help him move some lumber from the truck to the upstairs loft. He looked everywhere for the boy, to no avail, until finally he spotted Zeke sitting near the rippling lake at sunset, an open Bible in his lap. He was contentedly munching on an apple, a faraway look in his eyes.

"Well, there you are!" Scott blurted in exasperation. "Look, Son, I love you and I'm really glad you're so deep and all. But there's a time to pray and there's a time to move lumber. Right now you need to move lumber."

After ecstasy, the lumber.

✿ ✿ ✿

For most grown-ups I know these days, the unbalance in our lives is not the result of too little laundry. (I haven't seen the bottom of the laundry basket in 15 years.) Unbalance in our fast-forward world is more likely to come from a shortage of *ecstasy*—which I define as an overwhelming, heartlifting, yes, *emotional* response to God and all the large and small blessings He gives us to enjoy.

Now I'm not suggesting we live our life or make decisions based solely on feelings. I once heard James Dobson on the radio discussing the title of his book *Emotions: Can You Trust Them?* "I basically took a whole book," Dobson quipped, "to say, 'No, you can't.'"

What I *am* crying out for is balance. There's every good reason to squeeze all the joy we can out of the experiences God graciously grants us. I view this as the chocolate glaze on what would otherwise be plain pound cake days. Why eat plain cake when, with a little extra effort, it's so often possible to enjoy a gourmet delight? It's laundry hung in sunshine; duty dipped in joy. And I believe, by purposely incorporating certain activities into our lives, we can experience more jubilees of heart.

One day I was reading Alan Loy McGinnis's excellent book on the subject of romantic love, *The Romance Factor,* and ran across one passage that became a small porchswing epiphany for me. In it, Dr. McGinnis discussed the subject of creating the conditions for ecstasy in our life.

He explained that though some scholars believe that positive peak emotional experiences "come only as momentary visitations," others feel we have more control over feelings of joy than we realize. In fact, Abraham Maslow believed that "although we cannot summon such heightened awareness, we can create the settings that make them possible."

McGinnis cited the research from the classic study *Ecstasy in Secular and Religious Experiences* by Marghanita Laski. He said that Laski called the preconditions for joy "ecstatic triggers," then explained, "These circumstances are not to be confused with the experience itself, because they frequently occur without bringing about any heightened awareness. But they happen so often in conjunction with peak experiences that they are important to examine."

The most common joy-producing triggers are:

- Art, especially music
- Natural scenery
- Play and rhythmic movement
- Religion
- Discovery of new knowledge
- Creative work
- Beauty
- Childbirth
- Sexual love

(There are also antitriggers, such as the presence of crowds, commercialism, litter, the exercise of reason, brutality, war, and ugliness.)

As I read over this list of joy triggers, one Bible character leapt to mind: David. Flawed, tempted, emotional David. But oh, how God loved this passionate shepherd-turned-king!

In David's psalms and in his Old Testament biography, we see him incorporating so many of the triggers of ecstasy into his life: love of music and nature, the joyous expression of dance, a hunger to create and build beautiful things, an obvious enjoyment of sexual love (which, unrestrained, got him into major hot water), and adoration of the God who understood, appreciated, and loved (and sometimes had to forgive) David's zealous, passionate heart.

In fact, no other man in Scripture is given such praise by God as David, the man after God's own heart. In other words, God saw qualities in David that He recognized in Himself! Who can honestly examine the Scriptures from start to finish and not see a God rich in the full range of emotions? From devastation to ecstasy, His expressions of love, anger, hurt, jealousy, mercy, and, yes, passion fairly pulsate within the pages. Because God is emotional, He FEELS our pain and our buoyant joy—and to reduce Him to charts and logic and boxes so He can somehow be contained and confined all collapses the rich layers of our own createdness into the flatness of a robotlike existence.

Having grown up in a Bible Church where the intellect seemed somehow elevated as a superior part of the human psyche, I have come to believe that many of us with similar church roots may have missed just how deeply God desires to nourish and care for our *emotions* as well as our mind. We're top-heavy. Our heads are full—we know our apologetics and our hermeneutics. If the truth be known, however, our hearts are often found wanting. (This is also a common bane of left-brained, studious people, no matter what denomination—if any—you were raised in.) There was something refreshing about hearing Tony Campolo once exclaim, unashamedly, "I want to FEEL God!" Most of us, in fact, could use an infusion of heart-pumping passion!

I just saw the movie *Chocolat* yesterday and thought it a wonderful allegory of religion that had lost its appreciation for passion. The law-bound, religious stoics of the community had lost the color in their cheeks, the spring in their step. All they could focus on was a world of "don'ts," thinking they were pleasing God with their sacrifice. Enter lovely Vianne, who opens up a chocolate shop—in the middle of Lent, no less! And suddenly, everywhere this kind woman walks and talks, she leaves vivid, bright colors of grace, unconditional acceptance, and joy—along with irresistible treats of chocolate truffles or mugs of creamy hot chocolate.

She literally dipped the community in chocolate—and reminded them, by her life-giving presence there, that Jesus was not a bland divinity and a man without feelings—He was the God-Man who felt the full range of divine and human passion, who loved food and dancing and earthy, flawed people. In fact, I'm certain that Jesus would have thoroughly enjoyed good chocolate.

In her book *Passion!* my redheaded dynamic therapist-friend Roz wrote, "Instead of grabbing life with their bare hands and relishing it, people seem to be handling it with tongs."

Enough of too-careful living. Enough of settling for a "Less Wild God," as the authors of *The Sacred Romance* put it, and thus settling for less-wild lives in drab shades of grey and black. Time for reds and yellows and brilliant blues! Time for savoring rich, creamy *Chocolat* moments!

Time to put the tongs aside and dig into life with our bare hands.

For now, the laundry can sit and soak.

Ecstasy awaits.

*Heart, body, and soul are filled with joy....You have let me experience the joys of life and the exquisite pleasures of your own eternal presence.*

PSALM 16:9,11 TLB

# 11

# Music to Soothe the Savage Mom

Coffee with rich cream. Turn-of-the-century decor. Linen tablecloth, crystal, silver. Morning sunshine pours through the dining room's Victorian stained-glass window and halos the snowcapped mountains in the distance. And now, my husband of 20 years kisses me goodbye. There is a childlike gleam in his eye, for he is off on an adventure—a day of snow skiing alone without having to worry about me, the children, or another living soul.

I meet his eyes with a knowing wink for I too am anticipating several hours of delicious freedom. On the table in front of me lies a Belgian waffle dripping with butter and orange marmalade along with a local paper, a pen, and the journal I'm recording my thoughts in this morning. Near my left a handsome waiter (part-time ski buff) stands eager to keep my coffee warm and my breakfasting pleasant. I will spend the afternoon visiting and shopping among the interesting, laid-back people of Durango (or "Durangotangs," as they call themselves). It is the perfect romantic getaway experience: each of us doing what we love for the day, then coming back together in the evening for dinner, conversation, and, well, other things. Now I ask you, does life get any better than this?

Yes, in fact, it does.

For now the strains of Pachelbel's Canon in D are drifting and swelling from somewhere above and behind my head. Let Scott have his slopes with fresh powder, I'm having my own personal "Rocky Mountain High" inside the

Strator Hotel Restaurant, enveloped by this beautiful piece of music. Involuntarily, tears spring and fall as quickly as I wipe them from my cheek.

Pachelbel's Canon (or as my kids say, "Taco Bell's Canon") is a surefire tear trigger for me, transporting me to a memory so dear that I relive it again in my mind as if it were happening now. I can almost feel myself standing in a small chapel near the back of a beautiful sanctuary helping my little sister, Rachel, arrange her wedding train. Our mom, the other bridesmaids, and I are laughing and chatting when suddenly, the bride takes hold of her train—and the proverbial reins. Putting her finger to her mouth she whispers, "Shhhh." Then quietly, her dark curls glistening against ivory satin, black eyes shining, she says, "Listen. It's my wedding music. I want to absorb everything about this moment right now." We freeze, like a posed arrangement of Wedding Dolls, listening as the music of Pachelbel's Canon crafts this special moment into our collective memories.

"More coffee?" The waiter's question startles me back into the present.

"Yes, please, with cream and sugar." Sipping at the china rim, I pause to sigh, and realize this is not the first time I've felt transported—as if caught in a time tunnel—by this particular piece of music.

A few years after the day I watched my sister become Mrs. Rachel Scott St. John-Gilbert III (I know, I also think it's a bit much), I purchased a tape of classical music, pushed it into my car stereo and set out on my daily drive to pick up my children from school. Pachelbel's Canon began to play and in my mind, I was no longer in my station wagon. I imagined myself back in that stained-glass church watching my beautiful sister float out the dressing room door to the strains of this lovely music, down the aisle toward her groom. I could barely see the road, the sentimental tears were flowing so fast and so free.

When the song ended I looked up with a start and found I was in an unfamiliar town—I'd missed the exit to my children's school by over ten miles. The children looked bewildered when, 30 minutes late to pick them up, I explained, "I'm sorry. You see, I was at your Aunt Rachel's wedding five years ago."

Shortly after the "missed exit" experience I visited my sister at her home in Virginia. One afternoon we went shopping at a mall and wandered together into a music store. Suddenly, Pachelbel's Canon began playing over the sound system.

"Rachel," I whispered loudly, "listen!"

"Oh, yes," she answered, a smile of remembrance spreading, her dimples deepening. "It's my wedding song."

"I know, I know! Oh, Rachel, did I write you about the time I started listening to this piece in my station wagon when I was supposed to pick up the kids? I got so carried away with the music that the next thing I knew I'd missed..."

"Becky, you're starting to cry!"

"Oh, I know (sniff) you just have to ignore me. I do this. Wait a minute. I'm okay (pause). No, never mind. I'm losing it again..."

"Becky, it's okay. Settle down. Remember, you were going to tell me what happened in your station wagon?"

"Oh, yes. Well, I was listening to this Canon. Is this not the most beautiful music you've ever heard? Oh, dear. I don't think I can finish the story. I'm getting choked up again."

At this point a nearby group of milling people were beginning to stop and stare. Through my watery eyes and sniffs I looked at Rachel then at the small crowd around us, laughed, and using my best Jewish accent said, "I'll be all right. Just tawlk amongst yuhselves for a moment while I pull myself togethuh."

I never did manage to get the story out. Rachel gave up waiting for my sentimental tears to ebb and decided it would be more prudent to simply move me on down the mall towards the Sharper Image and Dillard's—significantly less emotional territory than a music store. I noticed she was also careful to steer me away from Things Remembered and Hallmark Sentimentals.

What can I say? I'm a sap when it comes to music. Especially romantic or patriotic music. Or bluegrass. Or soft jazz. Or those cute little kiddy songs on the "Wee Sing" or "VeggieTales" tapes. It's as if the notes enter my ears, go straight to my tear ducts, and yell, "Now! Turn on the faucets!"

Scott and I recently attended a banquet for about 300 Bank CEOs and their wives. I was invited there, believe it or not, to speak. (Yes, life is full of quirks: Author of *Worms in My Tea* meets The Banking Institution.) After my talk a musical troupe was providing the evening's entertainment. At its close, the lights came down low and one of the performers, a baritone, gently sang a moving rendition of "I'll Be Seeing You." Certain strains of the song brought sweet memories of my grandmother, Nonnie, into my mind and, predictably, the waterworks began to flow.

Honestly, I hate my "musical crying" personality disorder; it's so inconvenient. I'd love to simply appreciate and absorb a touching piece of music—perhaps wipe away a delicate tear—and be done with it. But I can't. For some reason, I flood. Because I was seated at the head table, there was no place to escape for a private tear-letting. After I'd soaked my napkin, Scott lent me his. Then a bank president's wife handed me hers. By the time I was dotting at my eyes with the corner of the tablecloth—the song mercifully came to a close.

Then the lights came up and there I sat, blinking at a sea of finance executives, looking like an overwrought raccoon. At this point, I'm sure Scott felt like saying, "Hey, I'll be seeing you, Babe," but he stood bravely by my side. At least until he had wiped the mascara from my cheeks, chin, and neck. Then he pointed me toward the lobby and disappeared quickly from view.

Once in the lobby, I ran into the sentimental crooner and began to tell him how deeply I'd been affected by his song. He was flattered, of course, at least until there was a short pause in our conversation and we overheard Scott, directly behind us, chatting with a lovely sequined soprano.

"Yeah, well," Scott was saying, as he chuckled amiably with the lady, "tell your buddy over there not to get a big head over any of my wife's compliments. I once took her and the kids to Show Biz Pizza and found her sitting at the table, sobbing all over her pizza because she'd just heard 'America the Beautiful' sung by a robotic gorilla."

Embarrassed, I whirled around on my heels and blurted, "Scott, that gorilla had really sincere-looking eyes!" So much for the baritone's brief moment of glory.

Music began wrapping its arms around me at a very early age. I think it started when I was in the second grade and my parents took me to see *The Sound of Music*. My eyes were wide, absorbing the opening scene: the incredible lush green Alps covering the entire length of the screen, and then Maria, her arms open wide to the heavens, twirling in childlike joy and singing at the top of her lungs. It dawned on me, for the very first time, that music comes from heaven and that we bounce it back.

A few Sundays ago words from the hymn, "And Can It Be," struck me anew: "My chains fell off, my heart was free. For O my God, [mercy] found out me." The hymn writer painted a word picture so intense that as the music pounded majestically from the organ and piano and congregation, the response of my heart to such an incredible gift increased—and of course, the tears poured. "Amazing love! How can it be? That thou, my God, shouldst die for me?"

A woman behind me—a fellow book/music lover—understood my predicament. She tapped me on the shoulder, split her Kleenex with me, and mumbled, "Good writing, isn't it?" Even recalling the hymn's words and humming the melody now causes tears to fall, fresh, down my cheeks again. Here in my office, in privacy, I don't mind the fact that my emotions hover so near the surface. It lets me know I am alive, that my child-heart is not calloused to His love. I never want to stop feeling. And I suppose I'd rather suffer the occasional embarrassment of being thought overemotional than have numb ears.

I believe if I could examine all the Bibles the world over and find the pages that are most rubbed and worn, the most tear-stained, and the most loved, I feel sure those pages would be from book of Psalms. Why? Perhaps because this book has been mankind's emotional echo—we find in its prose something that cannot be explained in logic. The Epistles satisfy our need for spiritual order and logic, but the Psalms have a way of bypassing our heads and embracing our hearts. I find it fascinating that throughout the centuries men and women have been most drawn to this musical book—this set of lyrical works originally intended to be sung and played rather than spoken, lyrics that have comforted us through untold sufferings as well as put words to our joy overwhelming. When I read a psalm, I like to imagine how it might have sounded coming from David's throat on a starry night, accompanied by the soft bleating of sheep and the peaceful strumming of his harp.

Out of curiosity one day, I decided to search out the first and last songs recorded in the Bible. What I discovered was like stumbling upon hidden treasure. The first song in the Bible is found in Exodus, chapter 15—the last song is in Revelation, also chapter 15. The first song is the song of

Moses, leading the children of Israel to freedom out of Egypt's slavery. The last? It is sung by saints who've triumphed over Satan's slavery and they are singing, get this, "The song of Moses the servant of God and the song of the Lamb" (Revelation 15:3). Isn't that incredible? The first and last songs in Scripture, both songs of freedom into light from a dark night slavery, are woven together in a majestic musical moment to end all moments!

Do you have a favorite spot on a tape, record, or CD you've nearly worn out over the years? Wouldn't it be fun to play our favorites for each other sometime? I have an odd, eclectic collection. I keep a James Taylor CD close by the kitchen sink for hummin' along with while loading the dishwasher. I absolutely adore a song by a boy's choir on Michael W. Smith's Christmas album called "All Is Well"—it melts me with a sense of childlike peace every time I hear it. I'm crazy about starting the morning with Art Garfunkel's (of the old Simon-and-group) CD for children (since I consider myself still one of them) called *Songs from a Parent to a Child*. My favorite wake-up-happy song from that CD is "Morning Has Broken." Kathy Troccoli's "Sounds of Heaven" is another well-worn favorite.

Oliver Wendell Homes said, "Take a music-bath once or twice a week for a few seasons, and you will find that it is to the soul what the water-bath is to the body." Since I'm a lover of hot baths too, I immediately understood the power of this suggestion.

In your darkest nights, in your brightest joys, in your most hum-drum days seek out and find your daily dose of music. It will cleanse and soothe your soul.

One of the sweetest passages I've ever read concerning an encounter with music came from Corrie ten Boom's book *Tramp for the Lord*. She described the day she was released from her torturous years in a Nazi concentration camp. Note how God used music as a way to bring out

Corrie's pent-up emotions—to allow her to fully express her relief and gratitude:

> Far in the distance I heard the sound of a choir singing and then, oh, joy, the chimes of a carillon. I closed my eyes and tears wet my pillow. Only to those who have been in prison does freedom have such great meaning.
>
> Later that afternoon one of the nurses took me up to her room where for the first time in many months I heard the sound of a radio. Gunther Ramin was playing a Bach trio. The organ tones flowed about and enveloped me. I sat on the floor and sobbed, unashamedly. It was too much joy. I had rarely cried during all those months of suffering. Now I could not control myself. My life had been given back as a gift. Harmony, beauty, colors, and music.

How about turning on some soft classical music at dinner tonight—even if dinner is McDonald's drive-through and you have to use your car stereo. Drag the guitar or banjo out to the porch swing this weekend and watch the neighbors come a'calling. Find a foot-stomping bluegrass, rock 'n' roll, or country song to help turn your vacuuming or dishwashing into a Housework Jubilee. (My friend, Suzie Duke, swears by Aretha Franklin for getting the housework done in a flash.) Or light a candle in the bedroom, turn on some sexy jazz, and watch your spouse melt into a lover.

And don't forget to bounce some music yourself, as a form of praise, back to heaven.

Sometimes a light surprises
The Christian while he sings
It is the Lord who rises
With healing in His wings.

**John Newton, "Joy and Peace in Believing"**

*David would take a harp and play it...then
Saul would become refreshed and well...*

1 Samuel 16:23 NKJV

# Musical Notes

Not only is music filled with spiritual and emotional meaning, it is good for our physical bodies. Consider the following tidbits:

- When music was provided in the critical care units of one hospital, they found that "half an hour of music produced the same effect as 10 milligrams of Valium. Also patients who had not been able to sleep for as long as three to four days fell into a deep sleep listening to music." (Take two arias and call me in the morning?)

- Elderly patients respond amazingly well to music therapy—they could recall every word to "Amazing Grace" even when they couldn't remember their own birthdays or hometowns.

Boy, do I believe this. In the year just before my ailing and fragile grandfather died, he exhausted a room filled with his children, grandchildren, and great-grandchildren by giving us all a thorough trouncing in the musical game Name That Tune. Granddaddy had played drums in a band from the '40s and had a reputation for being quite suave on the dance floor. It was an absolute delight to watch our aging, sickly patriarch perk up as he found new energy to whistle, sing, and even snap out tunes from his heyday.

- In one study when soothing music was piped into an operating room, the amount of sedative required by the patients was cut in half.

- When Brahms's Lullaby was prescribed for premature infants as part of an experiment, the results were incredible. The infants gained weight faster and went home a week sooner than the babies who didn't hear the music. A savings of $4800 per infant! (And, hey, you can buy a lot of concertos for 4800 bucks.)

## 12

# To Paint! To Dance! To Play!

**M**y mother-in-law, Beverly, who seems to be blossoming more and more the older she gets, paints vivid watercolors of nature that simply astound me. (She also took off to a little village in Italy this past summer to paint. How's THAT for following your passion?) A few years ago, before her paintings took on such a profound, professional quality, she told me about a book that inspired her called *Drawing on the Right Side of Your Brain.*

Now, the title does not mean we should take a Magic Marker to the right half of our noggins as it may at first imply. It means to enjoy creativity, we may have to begin by ignoring the logical left half of our thoughts and let the little kid "I'm-an-artist!" half run loose for a while.

If you ask any kindergartner, "Are you an artist?" they'll answer by saying, "Yes! I can draw anything. Whadaya want? A polka-dotted elephant? How about I color a picture of you?" (Then they draw a portrait of you that looks an awful lot like a polka-dotted elephant.)

Can you remember, way back when, how much fun it was to color and finger paint before grown-ups told us we had to stay in the lines? Or that trees should always be green and never, ever blue-and-pink striped? It's no wonder most of us finally gave up in defeat by the time we graduated from third grade declaring, "I must not be artist material."

I believe that God, the ultimate Creator, designed us with a natural desire to create. It comes with the territory of being made in His image. When we are intensely involved in a creative process, sometimes we're almost startled by the feelings of joy welling up within. When you think about it, haven't some of your happiest moments—when time ceases to exist—occurred during moments of intense creativity? If not, then perhaps it is time for you to scrounge up an old box of crayons or grab some charcoal pencils and a container of paint. Take them outside along with a thick pad of paper on some beautiful day and let yourself go.

Doodle clouds. Make thick paint strokes of the sunset. Color, for once, outside the lines! Or perhaps you might enjoy taking a pocketknife out to the porch and whittle a piece of wood. (Scott's into woodcarving right now. So far he's whittled a duck that looks remarkably like a fish, and a fish that looks remarkably like a duck. But he's havin' a ball and we're all getting a kick out of the results.) Or get some clay and try your hand at pottery or sculpting. It doesn't matter what form it takes as long as you enjoy it and as long as you are making something.

If you're having trouble getting started, I highly recommend bringing a five-year-old along for the afternoon. They will make you feel like a bloomin' creative genius. A typical five-year-old can always be counted on to say, "WOW! You're good!" Even when you just sculpted a horse that looks like a pineapple with hooves.

Children instinctively understand that play and art are intertwined. Once I had my nieces and nephews over and let them make their own little pizzas. I began by thawing a package of raw frozen rolls and then encouraging them to pat the dough into flat circles for the crust. But the sight of all that raw gushy dough proved to be too much.

It started with dough sculpturing. Then it blossomed into mask making: big fake noses made of dough. Dough glasses. Dough hairbows. Once things were already completely out of hand, Gabe looked at me and asked, "Mom, could we throw just one piece on the ceiling to see if it will stick?" I started to say no, then thought, *Why not?* and before I knew it dough balls were shooting ceiling-ward all over my kitchen. A few dough balls pulled loose and came down before we figured out you really have to put lots of muscle into the arm throw to get them to stick. There's an art, you see, to throwing dough on the ceiling.

Art takes a thousand different forms we may not recognize at first glance. For example, besides playing, painting, drawing, and sculpting, I believe that sports and athletics can often be seen as art on display—the medium just happens to be our physical bodies. There's something beautifully artistic about an athlete stretching well-trained muscles as he or she performs their sport with expert mastery. Inspiring scenes of athletic triumph from movies like *Chariots of Fire*, Olympian gymnasts hitting that perfect 10, or ice skaters gliding, like liquid silk, across the ice remind me of the magnificence of the human body in motion—a kind of fluid art. Of course, there are those of us who look more like poultry in motion than poetry in motion when it comes to athletics—but as long as there's joy in the performance and physical movement, it doesn't matter. It triggers ecstasy.

Dance is yet another example. My family, who could easily have won the Most Conservative Conservatives on the Block Award, had a healthy appreciation for dancing—for the pure simple fun of it. One of my fondest memories is pulling all the furniture back against the wall while my Aunt Etta and Uncle Jimmy taught us kids how to two-step, schottische, waltz, and Cotton-Eyed Joe until our toes had blisters or we pooped out from exhaustion. The kids, that is. Aunt Etta and Uncle Jimmy were never too pooped to party.

Pulitzer prize-winning author Annie Dillard fondly recalls her own childhood memories of dancing in the living room. "We did a lot of dancing at our house, fast dancing; everyone in the family was a dancing fool. I always came down from my room to dance. When the music was going, who could resist? I bounced down the stairs to the rhythm and began to whistle a bit, helpless as a marionette whose strings jerked her head and feet."

Even toddlers in diapers gleefully bounce to music pouring from a radio. So to me, dancing has always seemed a natural, physical, joyful response to music. I understand having problems with, say, erotic dancing in public, but I never really understood why dancing—across the board—has been labeled "evil" in some religious circles.

Just a few months ago, my mother was talking about having thoroughly enjoyed the movie *The Doctor.* "Becky," she said thoughtfully, "it was so interesting to me that the experience that finally brought this physician out of his shell of solemn control was a spontaneous dance out of doors with a cancer-stricken young woman to music coming from a car stereo. You know, I think people who've never danced are missing something of the joy in life." I tend to agree, having experienced, as I waltzed in my husband's arms, many times when we both felt we were floating on a cloud of ethereal, married joy.

One summer when Scott and I were newlyweds, we vacationed with my parents. We ended up in North Carolina visiting a Christian couple who had opened their home to several intellectual and artistic young college students. One of the girls kept telling us about how she loved to "worship the Lord with dance." Now, I could understand ballroom or kicker dancing, but I'd never given much thought to dancing as a form of worship, and frankly the whole idea seemed so odd that we all tried to change the subject whenever she brought it up.

Then one Sunday morning, during an outdoor informal worship time, this young girl walked out dressed all in black. Her feet were bare and she wore a long black skirt that flowed over black dancing leotards. I stole at glance at my mother, and she looked back at me as if to say, "Uh-oh. What are we in for here?"

I'll never forget what happened next. She walked out on the dew-covered grass and knelt—in the pose of prayer—under the limb of a bountiful oak tree. The sun glinting behind her strawberry blond hair gave off a brilliant glow. Then from somewhere behind us, music began to play and a baritone sang the "The Lord's Prayer." The young girl began to unfold like a tulip, slowly opening her arms, reaching toward heaven. With her body, she continued to interpret that beautiful prayer set to music in a way I wish to this day I could see just once more. It is hard to describe how lovely, how right, how worshipful that dance was. When I looked over at Mother, we were both wiping at our tears.

David danced before the Lord "with all his might" (2 Samuel 6:14). He wrote that God "turned for me my mourning into dancing" (Psalm 30:11 NKJV). Zephaniah 3:17 says that God "will joy over thee with singing" (KJV). The word "joy" literally translates to mean "jump and spin."

Jesus once compared himself to the flutist in a common children's rhyme that says, "I piped for you and you would not dance" (see Matthew 11:17). If Jesus plays the flute for me in heaven, I'd like to think I'd be one of the first ones out on the golden streets, dancing a jig of joy, celebrating the ultimate Homecoming.

❁ ❁ ❁

*When he came near the house, he heard music and dancing....."We had to celebrate and be glad, because this brother of yours was dead and is alive again."*

LUKE 15:25,32

# 13

# For the Beauty of the Earth

I t is the end of February, and we've had several seemingly unending days of rain—setting a new county record of "yuck." These are not the days of fresh spring showers, but dull gray-brown cloudy days of wintry-cold rain. People everywhere—at the gas station, restaurants, the kids' school, the neighborhood—can talk of little else but our mutual starvation. Our eyes have a gnawing hunger for light—the bright sunshiny kind. The kind John Denver sang about—warming our shoulders, making us happy. And we can't wait for our first taste of the brilliant green leaves we know are hidden somewhere in those colorless dripping branches. We long for nature's palette of beauty—one of the richest sources of feel-good joy in life. Who knows how many psalms, hymns, songs, and poems have been inspired by the sight of a mere leaf or blade of grass? Much less magnificent mountain ranges, waterfalls, or ocean waves?

To tide me over until I can soak up something alive and green, I've enjoyed watching some rented movies set in lush green English countrysides or exotic forest locales. A temporary fix, I'll grant you, but nonetheless helpful. These days I'll take what I can get.

According to the book *Healthy Pleasures*, "We have an appetite for such visual feasts." More than a luxury, research shows that "flooding our brains with rich natural visual stimulation helps us recover from surgery, tolerate pain, manage stress, and attain well-being." Not only that, but people the world over seem to have the same sort of response to beautiful natural scenes. "When people view slides of natural scenes, they report much higher levels of positive feelings such as friendliness and elation, and reduced feelings of sadness and fear than do people looking at manmade, urban scenes."

(Thought: Doesn't this make you wonder if we are going about the urban/violence crisis all wrong? Perhaps we don't need more police or gun control or special after-school programs. Maybe all we need to do is to haul truckloads of dirt and manure, filled with grass seed, to the downtown ghettos. Follow that up with a few cows, ducks, and pigs, hang a porch swing on every stoop—and voilà—instant friendliness and elation. Urban Jubilee. I don't know why the government doesn't consult me on these things.)

Thankfully, we can count on the world turning pretty and velvety when the sun goes down, no matter what season it happens to be. My husband loves to go out walkin' after midnight. In the moonlight. Even in February. It's earned him the nickname "Moonwalker."

On summer evenings, Scott's even been known to sneak out of the house at night, quietly row the bass boat out to the middle of the lake, stare up at the sky full of stars, and, if the water is nice, dive in for a refreshing dip. (This I can't quite bring myself to do. I've seen a water moccasin or two slithering out there. I've also observed they are dark in color and blend really well with lake water.)

Even though I won't swim with snakes, Scott and I often go for strolls together up and down our tar-covered roads. There's nothing quite like watching a night sky to put one's self back in perspective—be it from a boat, on a walk, doing the backstroke over the water, or dangling in safety from the front porch swing.

One of my all-time favorite relaxing-in-nature books is Anne Morrow Lindbergh's *Gift from the Sea*. It always brings me, mentally, to a warm, relaxing beach. It's a great book to read in the dead of winter! If, by chance, you are going to the beach anytime this year, I highly recommend you tuck a copy of this classic into your tote bag to unwind by. (After you've packed all of my books in first, of course.) In one chapter, Lindbergh recalls what to her has been a spectacularly perfect day.

She and her sister had escaped from their families to vacation together in a small cottage by the sea. They spent the morning and afternoon swimming, chatting, doing small chores, sharing lunch, and then each went their own way to write or read for a few hours. Coming back together again at dusk, Anne describes so beautifully the way Scott and I feel about nighttime:

> Evening is for sharing, for communication. Is it the uninterrupted dark expanse of the night after the bright segmented day, that frees us to each other? Or does the infinite space and infinite darkness dwarf and chill us, turning us to seek small human spark?

> We walk up the beach under the stars. And when we are tired of walking, we lie flat on the sand under a bowl of stars. We feel stretched, expanded to take in their compass. They pour into us until we are filled with stars, up to the brim.

> This is what one thirsts for, I realize, after the small-ness of the day, of work, of details, of intimacy—even of communication, one thirsts for the magnitude and universality of a night full of stars...

Or as the psalmist sang on solitary black nights, with sheep baaaaing softly in the background: "When I consider thy heavens, the work of thy fingers, the moon and the stars, which thou hast ordained; what is man, that thou art mindful of him?" (Psalm 8:3,4 KJV).

God's heaven and earth are waiting to be relished. Spectacular displays, free for the taking, are right outside our front doors.

I marvel at the beautiful detail, not only in God's creation, that went into the construction of His Old Testament dwelling place: the temple. Gold and silver; scarlet, purple, and blue cloth; jewels of all kinds; handcrafted woodcarvings.

The beauty of the earth, the glory of His temple: mere appetizers of the visual feast that awaits us in heaven—when we will behold His beauty with unveiled face.

"Let the beauty of the LORD our God be upon us...."
Psalm 90:17 NKJV

It finally came! Today I edit and add these sentences in the full blossom of spring! Sun on my shoulders, breeze in my hair, and green, green, green as far as the eye can see. Breathtaking. Even my cold toes are beginning to thaw.

Be encouraged, my friend. So many things we struggle with in life, like those dead-looking trees, take a little time to blossom into things of beauty. It helps us to relish and appreciate our springs when they finally arrive.

*He has made everything beautiful in its time.*

ECCLESIASTES 3:11

## 14

# Everything You Want to Know About Midlife Sex and Are Too Tired to Ask

**B**ecause Scott and I fell in love as teenagers in a Spanish-speaking country, we chose to celebrate our twentieth anniversary, five years ago, with a second honeymoon to the Baja Peninsula. One morning we woke up early and walked three miles to catch a city bus into the nearby town of Cabo San Lucas. Once we landed in this seaside "funky town" (as our native tour guide called it), we skipped the big city stuff, walked straight to the marina, and hopped a glass-bottom boat. Scott, ever the adventurer, convinced the boatman to drop us off at a remote beach. "I come back for ju in one hour," our guide assured us.

"No es necesario, " Scott answered brightly, his brown eyes sparkling with mischievous excitement as he scanned the nearby rocks and cliffs. "We'll climb our way back into town."

"Oh, no, Señor," the boatman argued.

"Oh, no, Señor," I echoed, looking first in disbelief at my husband and then imploringly at our water taxi driver.

"Becky," Scott said as he reached for my hand, "it will be fun. Trust me." What could I say? This was our second honeymoon. The last thing I wanted to do was start a fight. I smiled weakly and waved the boatman away, feeling as though I'd been abandoned on an island with a wild-eyed Gilligan as my only companion.

"Come on, Beck," Scott coached as he scaled one boulder after another as easily as a mountain goat.

"This is great! Look, you can see the whole town from up here!"

At first I was valiant, then merely good natured, then a bit cranky. After a half hour of nerve-wracking climbing, I finally lay prostrate on a rock and begged Scott to flag down our friendly boatman and let him row me back to shore. But he was having too much fun to even notice how far I was lagging behind. I squinted in the sun, sure I was seeing a vulture circling overhead.

Just then, a little old Mexican man complete with sombrero and gray mustache popped up beside me and said, "I help you, Señora." He was right on cue.

"Muchas gracias," I answered with relief, struggling to sit up. "Como se llama, Señor?"

"Pablo." Pablo! What a friendly little Mexican name! This was too good. With little old Pablo by my side, directing my every step, I finally caught up with my husband and an hour and a half later the three of us arrived in one funky piece in Cabo San Lucas. Every muscle I owned—and some I didn't know I had—shook from the exertion. I was filthy and exhausted and as thirsty as I'd ever been. I gratefully handed Pablo a handful of pesos for his trouble.

"Are...we...having...fun...yet?" I managed to ask Scott through my parched lips. "Sí!" Scott answered exuberantly, pointing toward an oasis. It was a luxury hotel, complete with soda fountain and bathrooms. After I'd splashed cold water on my face and downed a large Pepsi, there was still a part of me that wanted to be angry with my husband for putting me through the rock-climbing ordeal, but another part remembered it was his adventuresome spirit that I'd always found strangely attractive. I decided to be a good sport. He hugged me, grateful that I'd let him "play on the rocks" without putting up much of a fuss.

"And now," I said with a sweet smile, "it's my turn to choose the activity."

I marched toward an outdoor restaurant where I sat down at a table and put my feet up on the chair beside me, leaned back, and soaked up the sea breeze. We enjoyed a leisurely dinner as we watched the sun slowly set in the west. After paying for our meal, Scott glanced at his watch and yelled, "We've got five minutes to catch the last bus back to our hotel in San Jose del Cabo!"

Like two teenage kids, we linked hands and ran down the street, hollering at the bus to stop. We caught the driver's attention and breathlessly climbed aboard the crowded and lumbering vehicle, taking seats in the back.

As darkness settled Scott pulled me to him and with sudden clarity I knew again what had always been true: We were still two crazy kids in love. And like two crazy kids, we couldn't seem to keep our hands off each other—kissing and necking in the back of the bus. It was noisy and dark so we probably went undetected, but I'm not sure it would have mattered at that moment. We were anonymous American lovers on a rickety romantic bus ride down the streets of Baja.

After a while, we noticed things getting awfully quiet around us. We suddenly realized, with surprise, that we were the only ones left on the bus. Since I spoke better Spanish, we decided I'd better check on the situation. I walked up to the front, nearly startling the bus driver out of his seat, and asked, "Conoce la vía a San Jose?" which loosely translates to mean, "Do you know the way to San Jose?" (It took great restraint to keep from singing my question.)

"We pass San Jose tirty minutos ago," the driver answered.

"Woops," I answered in English. From the look on the driver's face, I gathered "woops" also translated well into Spanish. We did eventually manage to get back to our hotel that night, and have enjoyed more than one laugh about missing our stop because we—supposedly responsible adults—had been too busy making out in the back of the bus.

How can this be? Here we were: married, with children, both pushing 40.

My body is a mere figment these days of what it was when I was a thin, tan, and wrinkle-free bride. Wrinkles are no longer a stranger to this epidermis. Monthly I pluck at least one stubborn, fast-growing hair from my chinny-chin-chin. There is no denying the fact that four pregnancies also left their indelible marks. A two-piece bathing suit has been out of the question for more than a decade. For that matter, Bermuda shorts are even getting a little iffy.

So why—with this 40-something-year-old body—do I often feel sexier and prettier than I did back in my teens? It has nothing to do with looks, but I think it does have a lot to do with relaxing. And the realization that sexual attractiveness has much more to do with our attitude than our stretch marks—or lack of them.

Scott, though more handsome today than ever, is also seeing some telltale signs of aging in his body. Aching joints, some loss of his bulkier muscles, gray hair at the temple (which, I tell him, makes him look very extinguished). It's been a rude awakening—Scott's good looks have been something he's always counted on and gray hair has a way of making a man come face-to-face with old codgerdom (especially when they turn up in your ears and nostrils). Still, in many ways, I look forward to Scott growing older. For one thing, I want to show him that it is the man inside him, and not just his outer shell, that turns me on.

I'll admit it: I'm enjoying and looking forward to many more years of "old married love."

As long as couples continue to relax and grow comfortable with their changing bodies, and if they keep seeing lovemaking as a playful gift from the joyful God who created it—this growing intimacy can be one of life's most perpetual, regular joy-triggers and happiness-inducers. (And remember, though the frequency of married, sexual love may slow down as the years pass, there's a gourmet quality to this that can be savored. Like once-a-week steak as opposed to everyday tacos.)

Scott and I may not know the way to San Jose, but—like a pair of love-crazed kids—I think we'll always find a way to steal kisses. Even when we have to hobble to the back of the bus with our canes.

**May your fountain be blessed, and may you rejoice in the wife of your youth.**

Proverbs 5:18

# 15

# Input! Input!

I laughed out loud in empathy at a sign across the top of the bookstore's shelves. "When I get a little money, I buy books; and if there is any left, I buy food and clothes." The quote was attributed to Erasmus, and I could not have said it better myself. I too am a confirmed bookaholic.

I could stay happily locked up—for weeks—in a well-stocked library. As a matter of fact, if I had my dream vacation, it would be a seaside resort, perfect weather, and a blank check to Barnes & Noble.

Do you remember that little robot (No. 5) from the movie *Short Circuit?* He had an insatiable thirst for knowledge and spent a good deal of time going around saying, "Input, Input!" (Tough lines, eh?) If I were made of computer chips and wire, I'm convinced I'd be related to No. 5.

There are so many wonderful things waiting to be discovered between the covers (of *books,* that is, just in case you are still mentally transitioning from the last chapter's subject matter). No matter how tightly packed my schedule, I always seem to squeeze in enough time to read (or at least to skim) two to three books a week. A day without reading? Are you kidding! You may as well ask me not to breathe.

What do I read? Again, this reveals another quirky dichotomy. I love to laugh and much of my writing comes from my own scatterbrained, comical life. But most of my reading is serious in nature, contemplative and informative:

theology, philosophy, psychology, and of most recent interest, molecular biology. Real human beings, especially, and how we tick, hold a special, unending fascination for me.

I think this hunger for knowledge may have been inherited from my granddaddy. Granddaddy Jones lived at poverty level most of his life in an old broken-down house brushed gray and red with West Texas sand. I now realize he was somewhat of an eccentric, though I saw nothing unusual about Granddaddy when I was a child. He always wore the same thing: beige work coveralls and a hat. He smelled of hand-rolled cigarettes, sweat, All-Bran, and prune juice. He'd often tape messages to things around the house to let us kids know what could and could not be touched. Across a jar of his favorite pear preserves he wrote, "For my own personal use." But I thought he was wise, inventive, and completely wonderful. He thumb-tacked my school picture—the one with my headband falling off and a couple of front teeth missing—right at kid's eye level, smack in the middle of the kitchen wall. I loved him for that.

I remember going out to Granddaddy's barn (where he spent most of his days) and standing in complete awe of his surroundings. For everywhere the eye could see there were stacks upon stacks of books. There were so many, in fact, that they made thick mazelike walls that towered high above my head. In the center of this barn of books was an old, overstuffed chair, a lamp, and a pen—which Grand-daddy used to underline passages he agreed with or to scribble a silent protest.

Because I seem to have come by a love of learning naturally, it's encouraging to read that scientists are now discovering many benefits in keeping an active mind. For example, when we exercise our brain by learning lots of new things, did you know the synapses in our brain cells actually become more efficient? (No matter our age!) When we tackle something outside of our comfort zone of knowledge—let's say a computer nerd learns to play the violin—the neurons really go crazy, branching wildly. Learning something new every day, keeping the mind active into old age, is now thought to delay the onset of senility and slow the progression of Alzheimer's disease. (A great resource for this is a book called *Brain Longevity* by Dr. Dharma Singh Khalsa.)

With all the talk about exercise and controlling cholesterol, it's a little known fact that "a major study found that the number of years in education is a more important factor in determining risk of heart disease than all the other risk factors combined!" (So I'm wondering—does this mean I can lay around on the couch and eat bonbons all day and still be healthy as long as I'm reading *War and Peace*?)

Of all the reading I love to do, there's one book I've never outgrown. Like the pot of oil that fills up every time some is taken away, God's Word gets richer and deeper the more I read it. How many insights are there in those pages for me, as yet undiscovered? Even in the rereading of the most familiar stories—the ones I've heard since childhood—new truths continue to surface. The Bible represents the ultimate treasure hunt, and I love to go digging into its verses to see what precious gem I might uncover today.

Someday, when we retire, I want Scott to build me my own private Book Barn just like my Granddaddy Jones's. There I'll sit all day as I read to my healthy heart's content—with one minor adjustment: I want my barn to come fully equipped with indoor and outdoor porch swings.

✿ ✿ ✿

*God gave them knowledge and skill in all literature and wisdom.*

DANIEL 1:17 NKJV

## 16

# Holy Work

Now, my friend Mary loves small children; don't get me wrong, but she's always loved them in very small doses. So you can imagine my surprise when I found out that she'd taken a position this year as a teacher's aide working with preschoolers and kindergartners. Which brings me to another of Lahski's joy-producing triggers: Creative Work.

I could hardly wait till the clock hit four so I could call Mary and find out how her first day went.

The phone rang several times before she picked it up, and when she finally did, her voice had a tired, ragged edge to it.

"How was the big day, Mary?" I asked, hoping I sounded sympathetic and grateful my wide grin couldn't be seen via the phone line.

"Becky," she answered sleepily, stifling a yawn, "I tell ya, I just don't know if I'm gonna make it or not. I started off chipper enough this morning. I wore a denim jumper and apple earrings and a big bow in my hair—the whole kindergarten uniform. Even figured out how to mimic the 'happy' tone of voice the other teachers were using. But by noon I was already heading downhill."

"What happened?"

"Well, I found this little guy wandering the hall when it was time for our class to go out to recess, and this child was bound and determined to give me a hard time. He kept saying, 'I'm not going outside, Mrs. Johnson.' I was positive that yes, indeedy, he was going outside, and so after several seconds of this verbal tug-of-war I firmly escorted him by the hand out to recess."

"Good for you, Mary," I said with approval. "If you don't establish authority from the first day, you'll be struggling with it all year long."

"Yeah, well, that's not the end of the story. A few minutes later, outside on the playground, this same little guy comes up to me, tugs on my skirt, and says, 'Teacher, I don't want to be out here.' I was more than exasperated by this time. 'Look,' I told him, 'this is getting really old. Why don't you want to be out here?' Then very quietly he answered, ''Cause, Mrs. Johnson, I'm not in your class.'"

I laughed and tried to comfort my friend at the same time. "Mary, remember how many mistakes I made that first—and last—year I taught school? Just be sure and write this stuff down. You'll gather some great stories, and you know I'm a vulture for good material."

"So glad I can be of service."

"Want a piece of advice from a retired teacher?"

"Oh sure, Becky. You retired from teaching after— what?—ten long months of faithful service?"

"Touché. But this is one of the reasons I took early retirement—it was so hard for me to disconnect from 'teacheritus.' You'll see what I mean. You'll get so used to hearing yourself called 'Mrs. Johnson' and using that 'teacher voice' all day that it's hard to switch when you get back home to civilian life. Scott used to get so aggravated at me when I'd forget to change modes and start talking to the family as if they were a class full of six-year-olds. 'Family, we want our living area to be neat and clean, don't we? So let's pick up our socks and shoes for Mrs. Freeman by the count of three, okay? One, two…Uh-oh, someone doesn't have their listening ears on…'"

"Great. Maybe that'll happen to me too, but I don't know. By the end of today 'Mrs. Johnson' was not only losing her teacher voice, she was only allowed to have safety scissors. I keep repeating to myself, 'This job will be just like pregnancy. Nine months and it's over.'"

So went Mary's Day One. In all honesty, I never dreamed she'd make it to Day Five. As of this writing, however, Mary is on Day 45, and I don't think I've ever heard her sound happier and more fulfilled in a job. Yesterday she came over for coffee with her blue eyes sparkling as she chatted about a little Spanish-speaking girl who'd just come into the classroom straight from Colombia.

"Becky, it was so neat. The poor thing was crying, scared by all the new surroundings, and I was actually able to calm her using my high school Spanish. By the end of the day she was saying, 'Me gusta Señora Johnson mucho, mucho, mucho.'"

"Oh, Mary, she did not."

"Okay, she didn't. But she will. She will…"

Mary's remarkable transformation is just one example of what happens when people fall into work and suddenly realize a marvelous thing—they are needed. It's why Mother Teresa was able to smile and thrive in the most pitiful of conditions. She knew her life's work had meaning and purpose. "There are no great tasks," she said, "only small tasks done with great love."

Some have termed this phenomenon the "helper's high." Study after study has shown that people who are in the business of helping others are happier, healthier, and live longer lives. George MacDonald once said, "Nothing makes one feel so strong as a call for help." It's amazing how we rise to the occasion when we know our input will make a real difference in others' lives.

Those who see their career as having a positive impact on people's lives may not always have money, power, or prestige, but they are among the most blessed workers on earth. They have what I like to call On-the-Job Jubilee.

You've probably heard the true statistic about most heart attacks occurring at 9:00 A.M. on Monday morning. I was fascinated to discover that research showed job satisfaction to be one of the most consistent indicators of low risk for heart attack. Among the 14 positive factors that retard aging, a happy marriage is number one, with job satisfaction following close behind as number two. That's just one of the reasons it's vital that we pause and examine our life's work now and again.

Scott and I went to a folksinging festival one day and happened upon a couple named Jim and Suzanne. Jim, wearing a homespun shirt of pale blue, picked out a lively tune on his banjo. Suzanne wore a prairie-style dress in a matching shade and steadily strummed a guitar's strings. Together they were harmonizing to an old western song. Even older than Hank Williams Jr.'s father's songs.

What struck me peculiar about this old-timey couple is this: They were about the same age as Scott and me. And somehow, this 30-something couple was making a living playing ballads and folk tunes for schools and fairs around the country.

During a break, I cornered Suzanne and asked her if she had time to put her feet up and chat (by this time, I was bursting with curiosity).

"So Suzanne, I've just got to know—why is it you and your husband are making careers out of singing 'Tumbling Tumbleweed' when everyone else in our age group programs computers?"

"Well," she began with a smile, the metal on the bottom of her laced clogging boots clanking as she shifted in her chair. She swung her long dark curls behind her back and continued. "I was a college student in Virginia a few years ago, and one day I came across a book of old folk tunes and just fell in love with them—there were all these great songs from bygone days when people used to have sing-alongs around pianos and campfires and porch swings. I guess they touched a nostalgic nerve in me, and I knew I wanted to find a way to share them with others. Especially children."

"So this, what you're doing today, relaxing and jamming and singing old songs, is how you make a living?" Scott asked incredulously.

By that time Jim had joined our circle. "Well," he drawled, "we certainly don't own much. Our home's a travel trailer. But you know what we do have? We have time to enjoy each other's company. And there's nothing like singing to an audience of fascinated kids. It's a good life, all and all."

By the world's definition of success, Jim and Suzanne are not meeting up. Any good businessman will tell you that school children are not the best-paying audience. And where's the status of a house, nice furniture, cars, and fine clothes? What about prestige? Aren't those things necessary in order to achieve the American Dream of happiness?

In a fascinating book called *Why We Do What We Do,* I was astounded by a study focusing on the mental health of people who set their life goals around one (or all) of the three most popular extrinsic American values: money, fame, and beauty. Interestingly, the researchers discovered that people who aim for these goals turned out to be mostly unhappy and suffering from a variety of mental distresses. But those who chose careers that emphasized intrinsic values such as meaningful relationships, personal growth, and reaching out to help others lived happier, healthier lives.

Jesus said, "He who loses his life for My sake will find it" (Matthew 10:39 NKJV). It is in giving that we receive. Receive what? Money? Power? Prestige? No, the currency we're paid for doing meaningful work is joy.

Even a subtle shift in perspective about the work we are already doing can make a huge difference in our satisfaction with life. If a full-time homemaker realizes that she's shaping the lives of her children, building a marriage to last a lifetime, making a haven for others in need of refreshment—that what she does matters, and matters significantly—it elevates her work to a new level. Energy and creativity flourish. Wiping noses, having coffee with a girlfriend, taking the kids to the park, even changing diapers become an art form—if these activities are done with love, creativity, and a sense of purpose.

If a man pumping gas or someone working behind a counter can see their job description as "encouraging and helping people" rather than tickin' off hours on the clock just to bring home a buck, their "job" moves to the realm of "mission." When we take pride in doing a job well, no matter how menial it may seem—"doing small tasks with great love"—even mundane household chores can be an acts of worship and joy. (I wonder if my kids would like to perform several small acts of worship and joy, with great love, for me this week?)

Ever take a look at Jesus' Earth-Job description? Born in an animal stall, the son of a carpenter, He would spend three homeless years in ministry: walking dusty roads, bringing good news, and healing the hurting. His destiny would be to die an excruciating death on a cross between two thieves in order to rise again, laugh at death, and invite us to join Him in eternity. The rich, the famous, the beautiful ways to success are most notably absent. And yet, was there ever a man more full of wisdom, joy, and peace?

Jesus also helped others catch a vision for how they could help spread His message. As one writer put it so well, "Jesus kept laying his hand on unlikely people saying, 'You are needed,' and so awakened in them a transforming respect for their own lives."

What creative work has God given you to do? Where is He pointing right now and whispering to your soul, saying, "You, My child, are needed here." I urge you, as a fellow struggler in this area, to go forth in complete assurance whenever He says, "Follow Me."

The path won't always be easy, and sometimes it's downright painful, but ultimately it leads to On-the-Job Jubilee.

And me? Have I found my creative life's work, my Jubilee Job?

Well, that's another story for another chapter.

*I have brought you glory on earth by completing the work you gave me to do.*

JOHN 17:4

# 17

# Throwing in the Towel?

**W**riting the bulk of that last chapter on the joy of creative and meaningful work was lots of fun, but there was a time when I was faced with personally applying what I'd written—at a point when I was close to calling it quits.

That fateful January, about five or six years ago, I received a small pile of 1099 tax forms that added up to a total of—well, I can't tell you, but let's just say it was not in line with what I'd assumed I'd been worth. It was a sobering moment and still, when I think about it too much, I experience little depressing waves—akin to nausea—surging through my emotions.

In 1994 I was fresh from the New Author's Starting Gate. Somehow my mom and I found ourselves in the surprising position of being "bestselling writers." We were told by publishers and agents that having a first book from a couple of no-name women sell this well was like being struck by lightning (only we assumed what we were experiencing was a lot more fun).

Four years and four more books later, in 1998, I had given hundreds of interviews, had my "picture took" for the cover of magazines, wrote a monthly column, and appeared on a few national television shows. Every week I received letters from readers of my books or columns (which I faithfully answer. Except the ones from deranged prisoners, like the one I got this week with two enclosures: a Bible devotional thought and a cartoon of a raccoon pointing a machine gun—no caption. I just pass these on as quickly as I can to ministries for the deranged). I had what most people would deem to be a fulfilling and flourishing writing career. So what was the problem?

Here's the problem: When I added up the hours I spent at my dream career—the research, the writing and rewriting, and the hours of doing my part in "author publicity"—and then deducted the expenses of equipment, postage, office supplies, phone, and travel, I found I was putting in as much or more time and earning less than I earned as a first-year teacher. Actually, I was probably making less money than the school cafeteria lady. (Oh, shoot, I may have been making less than the kids in the cafeteria line!)

Bumping into that stark realization was something like biting into a chunk of baking soda in what had been, up to that point in time, a delicious chocolate chip cookie.

Which led me to the Big Question of the Year: Why, for goodness sake, should I continue to write? I needed to know clearly why I was doing what I was doing. So I sat and figured it out the only way I knew how: I read and wrote until the answer came.

One morning during this introspective period, my family awoke to below-freezing conditions—inside our house. During the night, a January cold front came in just as the butane went out. Scott—my frontier guy—braved the frigid air and took over the morning rush. While he helped our well-chilled children off to school, I turned my efforts toward thawing. Once the troops were gone, Scott strolled back into our bedroom and found me sitting upright in our bed, rubbing my hands together over a steaming cup of coffee. During his brief absence, I'd been dressing in assorted layers of turtlenecks, thermal underwear, socks, slippers, pajamas, and robes, and then I'd topped myself with a woolly hat and scarf. Propped up on my shivering lap lay Catherine Marshall's classic book *To Live Again*.

"Come on, Hon," Scott teased as he scanned the cover, "you aren't that bad off!"

Actually, I'd grabbed Mrs. Marshall's book because the title so perfectly fit my inner search du jour. I needed to find my bearings again, motivation to go on since discovering my 13-year-old daughter's baby-sitting business was more solvent than my freelancing career.

"Scott?" I asked, my sad eyes following my husband as he walked to the dresser. "Do you realize the paltry amount of income I contribute to this family?"

"Becky, you contribute things to this family money can't buy."

"Like what?"

"Well, you give us someone to make fun of, for one. Classy outfit ya got on there."

He pulled a pair of gloves out of the drawer and slid them on his hands. "Anyway, artists and actors and writers and stuff are famous for their paltriness. And you need to remember how many income-producing opportunities you've turned down because you wanted to stay close to home until the kids are older."

I clung to one word Scott had said. "So you think of me, then, as an artist?" I asked, pronouncing the word "ar-teest." I rubbed my nose to warm it, pulled the scarf up around my chin, lowered the cap over my eyebrows, and waited expectantly for my husband's response. He took a long, gentle look at me, then shook his head as if struggling, once again, to accept that he'd married a bona fide fruitcake. A frozen fruitcake, at that. Then he strolled out the door, closing it softly behind him. The only thing that kept me from collapsing in a heap of self-pity was the grin I caught on the side of his face as he took his leave. Unmistakable were the little rows of half parentheses on the side of his mouth—evidence that I, at least, still amused him.

Just then, the bedroom door opened slightly as he poked his head back in and announced, "Harold the Butane Man is here!"

"Great!!" I shouted, already anticipating the luscious warm air that would soon be wafting again through the vents. Then I remembered something about The Butane Man that brought a fresh deposit of depressing thoughts to my freezing and fragile emotions.

"S-s-cott," I said, my teeth chattering as I talked, "d-d-do you r-remember that t-time, about f-four years ago, when H-h-arold came over to f-fill our butane t-tank and I was so excited a-b-bout *Worms in My Tea* that I r-ran up to his truck, sh-showed him a copy, and t-told him I was an author?"

"Oh, yeah. Isn't he the one that told you not to quit your day job?"

"Uh-huh. When I t-told him, 'It's t-too late, H-harold, I already d-did,' he looked so stunned." I drew the blankets tightly to my chin and leaned back on the pillow. "M-maybe Harold was r-right. Maybe I sh-should have kept a d-day job."

"Becky, look—you have a day job. Okay, I'll say it: You are an ar-teest. A rather paltry breadwinner, I'll grant you, but a magnificent arteest. And God's meeting all of our needs, isn't He?"

I gave my husband half a smile as he went outside to greet Harold. *What am I doing?* I silently asked the book in my hand, flipping its pages in search of some comfort. *Should I keep writing in faith, or jump track now and get myself a real job with a uniform, benefits, a steady paycheck, hot meals on a plastic tray—and maybe even one of those nifty hairnets thrown in?* I was running dangerously low on pep-thoughts.

**And the soul of the people became very discouraged on the way.**

Numbers 21:4 NKJV

## 18

# Writing Back to Life

I turned to the chapter Catherine Marshall had titled, "Work for the Hands to Do." My eyes were drawn to a passage Mrs. Marshall had quoted from a book she'd read as a little girl—a book called *Emily of the New Moon*. In the book, a teacher asks Emily (who yearns to be a writer), "Tell me this—if you knew that you would be poor as a church mouse all your life—if you knew you'd never have a line published—would you still go on writing—would you?"

"Of course I would," came Emily's disdainful reply. "Why, I have to write—I can't help it...I've just got to."

*I can't help it... I've just got to...* Like Emily, like Catherine Marshall, like most writers who love their work, I did not begin writing with a paycheck in mind. I started writing at age 11 because I simply couldn't help it. My mind would be all a'muddle, my thoughts in knots, and it was through writing I found I could untangle the knots, lining up the pieces until eventually they would take on meaning.

Little about professional writing, however, has been as carefree as those childlike pouring-it-all-out-in-my-diary days. I'll never forget the agonizing months of waiting after Mother and I mailed off our first manuscript (for *Worms in My Tea*) to a list of publishers. How we'd find an editor's letter glinting in the mailbox, hold it to our hearts, dare to hope, and then—watch that hope splatter as we'd read things like: "Dear Mrs. Freeman and Mrs. Arnold, we are sorry...but we simply cannot publish books with worms wriggling through the text" or "What a coincidence! We already have six similar projects involving black tea and gray invertebrates" or "This is really funny, but alas, as we both know: you two are nobodies. If you get a big television or radio thing going, give us a call."

During that difficult waiting/rejection period, I happened upon a comforting chapter in Madeleine L'Engle's memoirs, *A Circle of Quiet*. In it L'Engle describes a painful day, her birthday, when she'd received the last in a long series of rejection letters:

> So the rejection on the fortieth birthday seemed an unmistakable command: Stop this foolishness and learn to make cherry pie.
>
> I covered the typewriter in a great gesture of renunciation. Then I walked around and around the room, bawling my head off...Suddenly I stopped, because I realized what my subconscious mind was doing while I was sobbing: My subconscious mind was busy working out a novel about failure.
>
> I uncovered the typewriter....

This is the fate of all destined-to-be writers: We cannot *not* write. (By the way—the wait, for Madeleine, finally paid off royally. She went on to win the Newberry Award for *A Wrinkle in Time* and has been prolifically published, with numerous accolades, over the years.)

There is another drawback to writing: It has a sneaky way of taking over your life. Ever the observer, I sometimes long to participate more fully in life's moments without constantly wrestling behind-the-scenes thoughts like, "This is such a special, tender moment. Wonder where I could use it?" or "This entire dinner conversation could be worked into my chapter on..." And I'm always near panic when someone says something adorable or profound and I'm caught without pen and scratch paper.

I had to laugh out loud at Susanne Lipsett's observations on *Surviving a Writer's Life:*

> You mean life is more than material for books? There's only one thing to do when you find yourself posing that question: stand up, walk away from your computer or your writing desk, and plunge your poor, steaming head into a bucket of ice water. Then lie down and let the sun dry you slowly while you think about nothing at all.

Often, in order to disconnect from my writing world and phase back into the real one, I've had to physically push myself away from the computer and march my legs out to the porch swing. Once there, I'll watch leaves dancing overhead or squirrels fussing over an acorn, allowing the wind to stroke my face until I'm generally calmed and my bogged-up head begins to unclog.

Another thing: Writing is hard work—REALLY hard work. If only writing would stretch and exercise my body as it does my mind—and my fingers. I have incredibly strong, lean fingers from all the typing I do. The circumference of my fingers is as tiny as a child's. My posterior, however, is another story. And, no, I shall not discuss its current circumference.

The surprising discovery that writing is hard work eliminates many a would-be player from the game of writing professionally. The spaces along the road to Published Land are often dotted with disappointment.

My Aunt Etta, our family's first published author, continues to write and teach to this day, but she offers no illusions about the stamina it takes to jump into the writing pool. Often, she opens her writing courses at Texas Tech with the famous analogy: "Writing is easy. You just go to your typewriter and open a vein." The glamour of writing fades quickly when confronted every day with a blank computer screen.

"I know some very great writers," writes author Anne Lamott, "writers you love who write beautifully and have made a great deal of money, and not one of them sits down routinely feeling wildly enthusiastic and confident. Not one of them writes elegant first drafts. All right, one of them does, but we do not like her very much. We do not think that she has a rich inner life or that God likes her or can even stand her."

I must also confess that I rarely skip to the computer—the sound of cheerful tweety birds singing in the background—bursting to capture my overnight profundities. I take the long way around to actually writing. I make coffee. Check my e-mail. Pour the coffee. Pick lint off the couch. Call a friend. Sip the coffee. Stare at the computer and wish it away. Refill coffee cup. Resign myself to the computer. Worry I'll have nothing of consequence to say, then dive in and write anyway. Once my motor gets cranking, the words finally start to flow. Unless they don't. Then I make more coffee.

Even when words are finally on paper, it is only the beginning. "Writing IS rewriting!!" our collective English teachers declared. Unfortunately, they were absolutely right. There is no shortcut, and every chapter I write, this one included, will undergo at least five to ten rewrites. Even then it won't be perfect. Improvements can always be made. This is why deadlines are a writer's salvation. Otherwise we'd never declare a piece "finished"—we'd write books that never end. Today, my daughter's teacher told her, "Writing's never done, it's just due." How true!

Let me pause for a moment here and add up what I've placed on the writing table thus far: Writing often pays pre-

cious little, it is hard work, the dailiness of it is unglamorous, and it is teeming with heartache and rejection (not to
mention that it broadens certain horizons one does not
wish to have broadened). What other career, other than
acting and painting, holds forth such an array of question-
able benefits? And more to the point, what is a nice girl like
me doing in a profession like this?

I love it.

I love it when I write something I know is good—really,
really good. So good in fact that I stand back in awe, click
my tongue, and am compelled to pat my own self on the
back. "Girl," I'll say aloud, "where did that come from? Who
poured those words through your mind? Composed them
so beautifully?" There's the fleeting impression—every so
often—that writing is something beyond myself, that perhaps it truly is a gift from above. I also know that a gift, if
kept wrapped and stored in some dusty corner, is never
fully enjoyed. It must be taken out to the light, unwrapped,
and shared. Even if some reject it, or don't like its texture or
color or style, it still needs to be offered up.

The joy that comes when your written words are not
only received, but appreciated, is near to the joy of birthing
a child. I keep every note of encouragement—they are
mega vitamins for low self-esteem, a tonic for my timid
soul. One letter I keep handy says, "There is nothing in this
world aside from sleeping and eating that I love so much as
laughing—and that is the gift I thank you for. My husband
is truly sleep deprived though, as I have read most of your
books aloud to him in bed. When I wasn't reading out loud,
I was laughing myself sick. If he sees another one of your
books in the house he may leave me."

Another precious note arrived, not long ago, on a day
when I needed a writing lift. "Last summer while on vacation I bought my first Becky Freeman book. What a joy! I

laughed and cried, sometimes at the same time. Don't stop writing. God has certainly given you a tremendous gift to bless His children with. Keep listening to Him and He will direct your paths." Don't stop writing. Keep listening to Him. Laughing is a gift I thank you for. God has given you a gift to bless His children with.

Now I ask you, honestly, how many jobs in the world offer benefits like these? What a blessing it is to know my feeble attempts at conveying a message actually touch the hearts of strangers—people I'd never meet without the miracle of the printed word.

Then, there is another joy. The joy of passing on the torch. Every week I see or hear of a talented new writer who just needs a little nudge to get them going. Several of them are now published. I'm especially good at encouraging new writers because they come to know me "just as I am"—and I honestly think they leave shaking their heads and saying to themselves, "I do believe if ol' Becky can write books, I ought to at least give it a shot!"

The people I've met, and the friendships I've made with authors and editors and publicists has been another unanticipated delight. If I never wrote another word, as a result of this career, I'd have made fascinating friendships that will last a lifetime. What price can you put on new friends? (As my charming Mary Engelbreit calendar proclaims, "Old friends is best, 'less you can catch a new one that's fit to make an old one out of." I've catched me a heap of new friends, these past few years, more than fit to make old ones out of.)

Why will I keep writing? Because I can't *not* write. Because it would be wrong to keep a God-given gift under wraps. Because I am thrilled every time a reader opens my gift and lets me know it was just what they needed and hoped for. Because there are other talented writers out there who need to be encouraged, whose stories need to be told, whose gifts need to be polished and made ready for giving—and I want to be there to squeal with them when they sell their first story. Because when I am discouraged and don't know if I can keep going, it is other writers whose hard-wrought words lift my spirit and remind me that writing is more than a paycheck, sales figures, and bestseller lists.

Writing, especially under pressure to perform, is not always fun. But writing to life—letting your words run wild and free—can be pure Jubilee. Everyone can unwind their mind with this sort of writing. Actually, this is the most healing of writing forms: simply allowing our thoughts to flow out and on to paper—thoughts that we may never share with another breathing soul.

My favorite and happiest times of writing are the simplest. Days when I take notebook, pen, and Bible out to my Porch Swing Place and write what comes to mind as I soak up the sun. It's also nice to snuggle up on the couch with notebook and pen during the cold winter months, but there's something especially peaceful about writing in the warm out-of-doors. Here's a sample from an old notebook, dated October 1994:

> *If ever there was a Norman Rockwell picture,*
> *this is it. I lie here on the dock observing Autumn*
> *make her gentle descent on lake and woods.*
> *Touches of scarlet and gold—early gifts—adorn*
> *the foliage. A large crappie somersaults above*
> *the lake and disappears in an instant.*
>
> *Three boys, one 14, the others about age eight,*
> *move along the shore in excited murmurs.*
>
> *"Put it here."*

*"I saw somethin' move."*

*"Can I hold it now?"*

*"It" is a net. Apparently it is the lone (therefore highly coveted) net for catching a school of minnows and other unseen lake dwellers. I peer to see who wields control of the handle. Yes…I see there are decided advantages to being the Big Kid.*

*As the afternoon sun plays about the boys and warms my outstretched legs, I squint my eyes, nearly closing them—but not quite. As I do, there's a hint of timelessness about this whole scene. Everything takes on an otherwordly glow.*

*If I should die before I wake from the nap I'm about to take on this wooden pier, I could say I left this world satisfied. After all, I've tasted the best of earth's bounty in moments like this.*

And so I kept reading and writing until the answer came, the waves of nausea subsided, and I could feel myself more at ease and sure that I was about the task God had given me to do, and He would care for our family's needs.

And I put off that day job a little while longer.

Update: After this chapter first appeared in *A View from the Porch Swing,* a friend, Cheri Fuller, who knew of my desire to keep writing without going bankrupt, introduced me to Greg Johnson, who has since become my literary agent and faithful friend. I also met Carol Kent, who mentored me in speaking, and added me to her speaker's bureau. Under Greg and Carol's guidance, God began opening door after door to provide for our family's financial needs and help us to pay off debts and occasionally even get ahead! With kids now heading off to college and getting into cars (and the accompanying fender benders), we are supremely grateful to FINALLY be able to say that writing has become a profitable venture.

To new and "wannabe" writers, I want to offer you some personal hope and encouragement, a new version of a country refrain that my sister scribbled and sent to me during the time I thought I'd be forced to give up my beloved writing career.

> *Write like you don't need the money,*
> *Write like you'll never get hurt,*
> *Write when nobody's reading,*
> *It's got to come from the heart*
> *If you want it to work.*

### Fan into flame the gift of God.

2 TIMOTHY 1:6

# Part IV

# Down-Home Hints to Health & Happiness

## A Potpourri of Laid-Back Musings

# 19

# Gourmet Napping

**M**y friend Linda, who is a busy mother of three boys and a physical therapist, leaned forward over the restaurant table where we were having lunch. "Becky," she said in hushed tones, "the other day I drove up to this dangerous-looking neighborhood to do a home visit, and as I walked toward the front door, I thought to myself, 'This is the kind of neighborhood where I could get shot. What if I do get shot?!? What if I get splattered by gunfire right here on the front lawn?'"

Using my best "isn't that special?" Church Lady imitation, I smiled sweetly and replied, "Well, there's a cheery little thought-for-the-day."

"That's the point, Becky," Linda replied, her eyes growing wide. "To me, it WAS a cheerful thought! Because my reflex response to my own question was, 'Hey, if I get shot, at least I'll have a good excuse to lie down and put my feet up for a while.'"

I laughed and said, "Look, Linda, I'm no psychologist, but I'd venture to guess that when a gurney starts lookin' like a cozy spot to curl up, it's time for a blankey and a pillow and a nice, long nap."

To Freud's eternal question, "What does a woman really want?" I answer, "She wants a nap. That's all, she just wants a nap." How many of you, I wonder, can identify with this? (If you are pregnant or have a baby or preschoolers, forgive me for even asking. I know, I know. The fact that your eyes are open long enough to read this sentence is a miracle in itself. I'm just honored that you're still with me.)

I used to think I didn't have time for such luxuries. A nap? Are you kidding? In the middle of my hectic day? Puh-lease. Or I might take one, but wake up feeling frazzled and guilty. There was always this fast-forward tape going on in my head, taunting me with a singsong, "You're getting behind-er, you're getting behind-er." I thought if I just kept doing and doing, staying focused on my to-do list no matter what—or who—interrupted my day I could actually, eventually catch up.

Then one bright morning, I had this incredible lemonade enlightenment and realized The Truth. There is no such place as "All Caught Up." It only exists out there in our imaginations with Oz and Santa's Workshop and Never-Never Land.

Why didn't the grown-ups tell us this when we were kids? I don't know, I simply don't know. Perhaps they too are still struggling under the illusion that it exists some-where out there. You may have to grieve a little over the loss of this fairy-tale catch-up land. You'll find it a healthy, cleansing experience, though. Because in the long run, I guarantee you'll be thankful I told you the hard truth right now, before you waste any more time chasing a dream. When you give up on the existence of "All Caught Up," you are free to do all those wonderful things you were waiting to do until you arrived there. Like, for example, taking a guilt-free nap.

I have learned, the hard way, that taking a short nap is the best thing I can do when I'm plagued with hurry-up-itis. I used to cram, pray, recite, and practice before a speech. Now I look for a good place to snooze for 20 minutes instead. I'm convinced God goes inside our brains and cleans house in there when we resign control of the universe long enough to let go and drift into a short sleep.

I've actually elevated napping to a gourmet experience. Let's say it's a springtime afternoon loaded with deadlines, housework, phone calls, and a hundred obligations, and I begin to feel the pressure building inside. (I love the title of Julie Barnhill's new book *She's Gonna Blow!* Any woman who's been there knows what built-up tension feels like and how everyone around you can pick it up.)

Like a movie producer who yells, "Cut!" I've learned to stop, walk away from the middle of the action, and melt like a boneless chicken into my quilt-laden hammock.

I soak up the warmth of sunshine on my skin and watch the play of light on the leaves in the trees overhead. Then I imagine my brain is a lot like the world before God fixed it up: dark, formless, and void. Very void. And I pray, "Father, hover over me the way You hovered over the formless deep, and create order out of the chaos that is now my mind."

As I imagine myself cocooned in His Spirit, I almost always fall into a deep, peaceful sleep. Then I wake up, in a few minutes, refreshed, without a trace of guilt.

CAN YOU BELIEVE IT? Trust me, this sort of experience has been a long time in coming. Now there are books on Power Napping, and even corporations are beginning to create Napping Rooms—realizing that the long-lasting effects of 15 minutes of rest are more effective than caffeine infusions from the coffee station.

"How can I stop for a nap when I have so much I should be doing?" you may ask. Here is the answer. You get three times as much accomplished in one well-rested hour as you do in three hours of plodding along half-awake. Take an hour to sleep and an hour to work, and you gain a whole extra hour to play with. Okay, I'll admit I just made that up. But you're just going to have to trust me on this one.

For you more scientific types, I do have some objective research proving that one nap a day will increase the number of your highly creative periods. It has to do with hypnapomping and hypnagogging. Really. I'm not making this up.

I know that hypnapomping and hypnagogging sound like disco dance moves, but they are real honest-to-goodness scientific terms used by sleep researchers.

Hypnapomping actually refers to that period of time just before we are completely awake, when our mental pictures are a mixture of dream and our own created images. It is considered one of the most productively creative periods. Hypnagogging, on the other hand, is that time just before we are asleep. Again, it is when images are a mixture of dreams and thoughts under our control—another highly creative state of mind.

Thomas Edison had an unusual technique for putting that hypnagogic state to work. "He would doze off in a chair with his arms and hands draped over the armrests. In each hand he held a ball bearing. Below each hand on the floor were two pie plates. When he drifted into the state between waking and sleeping, his hands would naturally relax and the ball bearings would drop on the plates. Awakened by the noise, Edison would immediately make notes on any ideas that had come to him."

I wish someone would explain why, if we are such a brilliantly advanced nation, American forefathers let the concept of a Nationwide Nap slip through the cracks of the Constitution? I appreciate that Ronald Reagan took naps while he was president. I, for one, miss having him in the Oval Office relaxed enough to take a little snooze now and then. His mere napping presence was soothing. (After all, if the president could nod off, what was there for the rest of us to worry about?)

In Latin America, they deal with midafternoon slumps by embracing The Siesta. The English have a countrywide sleepy-time breather they disguise as a tea party. Again, it takes place in the late afternoon and, because the English are the way they are, they call it High Tea. One of England's most celebrated citizens, William Shakespeare, penned the poignant words, "Oh, beloved nap time, nature's soft nurse."

Indeed, a short sleep is a healing balm.

Now, if you'll excuse me, the birds are tweeting outside my office window, the quilt-covered hammock is calling—and so off to hypnagog I go.

### I will lie down and sleep in peace.

PSALM 4:8

# Sleep Trick

I will admit, for young mothers and women with out-of-the-home jobs, this is not as easy to pull off—but with a bit of finagling you too can nap in the sunshine in guilt-free bliss. At least occasionally, or in modification. Young mothers can set up playpens outside in the backyard on beautiful days, lay the baby down to sleep in the shade, and catnap nearby on a lounge chair. Toddlers are tricky though, a real dilemma for their sleep-deprived parents.

Speaking of toddler tricks, did you read about the man who woke up from a nap with a sudden loss of hearing in one ear? True story. He went to the doctor to find out what happened. Turns out this guy's two-year-old put superglue in Daddy's ear while he was snoozing away on the couch. Aren't preschoolers just too precious? The only way I know for parents of toddlers to get a deep, peaceful nap is to hire a wide-awake baby-sitter, preferably with Olympic energy and a high IQ, to stand guard for you. I've heard rumors that in previous generations mothers would give their little tikes a dose of Paregoric to knock 'em out for a couple of hours. But that might get you arrested today. (Of course, there are days—for parents of toddlers—when a nice quiet jail cell sounds unbelievably enticing.)

## 20

# Pet Therapy

It had been a long, hard summer without a shower and shave. Colonel was beyond needing a homemade, garden-variety haircut: It was time for a professional barber. Or a groomer, as they call it in the doggie world.

So early one morning I dropped our miniature schnauzer off at Country Kennels Grooming Salon to see if they could salvage what was left of him. When I went back to pick him up, I could hardly believe the transformation. There on the grooming table stood a champion of a dog: his back shaven close, his silvery "skirt" combed out like silk, the irresistible dark eyes peering beneath bushy eyebrows, his snout adorned with the classic schnauzer mustache.

"I can't believe it!" I shouted. "Colonel looks fantastic!"

"Oh," said the lady, shaking her head. "That's not Colonel. Here's your dog."

She opened one of the cages to let a sad-looking animal come slinking out. As I gently lifted my pitiful pet to my arms, I couldn't help but comment, "He's naked."

"I'm sorry, Mrs. Freeman," the lady across the counter said kindly. "We did the best the best we could. His hair was so matted and tangled we basically had to shave everything off. We are dog groomers, not miracle workers."

I paid our bill, then Colonel and I hung our heads and walked out the door in shame. I vowed never to let a dog of mine go through such a humiliating experience again.

So now I scrounge up the money to have Colonel professionally groomed at least once every two months. And yes, it's worth it. These days he's holding his furry schnauzer snout high, his silvery/black skirt is combed silken soft. Most evenings, Colonel sits in my lap as I stroke his fur and talk baby talk to him. In spite of myself, a mutt has wrapped himself around my heart. An animal has turned yet another human into a blabbering idiot. (At the doggie barber, they refer to me as "Colonel's Mommy.")

Daisy, our eight-year-old rust-and-white Brittany spaniel, is also tugging at our heartstrings these days. We've never owned a pet long enough to see it age. They've always met with an untimely death, usually in the prime of their life. (There was the unfortunate kitten that fell into the fan belt; various animals that have fallen beneath car wheels; Rachel's rat that committed suicide by jumping out of its cage into Colonel's mouth; and that one awful time I accidentally blew up Zeke's ferret by feeding it leftover Mexican Casserole.)

But Daisy's been a true survivor of the Freeman Family Farm. So it astounds and saddens me to realize that almost overnight Daisy's gone from a young marathon rabbit chaser to a dog-bed-bound old lady. Her hind legs shake with arthritis; her great happinesses are sleeping, eating, and getting her belly rubbed. Gone are the days when she challenged every passing car to a race. "Ah, let 'em win," she seems to say as she rests her head on her paws and lazily watches them pass. I don't know when it happened, but sometime this year Daisy bequeathed most "car chasing duties" to her chipper subordinate, Colonel. However, Daisy isn't so old that she'll let Colonel have her bed. Not that he hasn't tried.

Colonel's been coveting Daisy's large dog bed for months. Everytime Daisy rises to get a drink of water or go outside to relieve herself, Colonel makes a mad dash for Daisy's king-size sleeping quarters. Feeling sorry for Colonel, I bought him his own bed. But no, this would not do. I came home one day to find Colonel sitting content-edly in Daisy's bed again. His bed? He ate it. Pieces of fabric and foam lay strewn all over the house.

"Colonel!" I scolded. "That's it. You are not getting another bed of your own. And guess what? You can't have Daisy's either! Now OUT-SIDE!"

I'm telling you, living with these two is like having little kids again. (Except that one of them is old and arthritic.) But I cannot imagine our household without these dogs. I was ecstatic to see them when they came bounding up the morning after their disappearance when I thought the bur-glar had got them. (Apparently, since we abandoned them for the day, they enjoyed an overnight Thanksgiving stay with another family in the neighborhood just as Scott had supposed.)

Colonel was recently attacked by a larger dog and ended up spending a night in the hospital suffering from a nasty bite, along with humiliation and shock. (The vet insisted Colonel was depressed, but when we got him back home, he jumped out of the car and marked all ten trees in our front yard. It was as if he were saying, "I'm back and I'm in CHARGE again.") Now these "strictly outside animals" have become lap-sitting babies. From pets to parts of our family. I've never considered myself more than an "animal liker," but in my old age, I have to admit I've been won over. I'm fast on my way to becoming an animal lover. Thankfully, I hear this is good for my health.

According to medical studies, "among people who suffer a heart attack, pet owners have one-fifth the death rate of the petless." (Of course, the studies don't say what caused the heart attacks in the first place. I'd wager a few of the pet owner's attacks happened when they discovered Fifi's unwelcome pet deposit on their new lace bedspread.) The benefits appear to come, not from increased exercise (you don't walk a pet lizard or fish), but in communicating with animals, stroking them, or just gazing at fish swimming in their tank. Pets also make us healthy in other ways.

First, they give recovering patients a living, breathing entity to get well for—because animals need their owners. Second, "having a pet provides moments of pleasure and solace in hard times, and a pet's compelling needs can interrupt our bad times. When the dog has to go out, out goes an ongoing argument, too." (I wonder if marriage counselors know this. They could train Divorce-Busting dogs—like they do Seeing-Eye dogs—that would automatically bark every time a couple had a twinge of irritation in their voices.) Third, pets give us unconditional acceptance. They love us in spite of the fact that we let their hair get wet and matted (and we also love them in spite of the fact that they chew up their new dog beds).

Animals also make fascinating study. I enjoyed listening to a tape series on "The Secret Life of Dogs." Granted, much of this author's musings are highly speculative—it's a virtual canine soap opera—still her intensive study of dogs and their habits made me much more aware of how intelligent and curious animals can be.

Gerry Spence, country lawyer and author of *How to Argue and Win Every Time,* says he's learned more from his dog than from most people. For example, when Gerry's dog wants some affection he asks for it—he just puts his head in the author's lap and gazes into his eyes until he gets some strokes. I need to remember to try this with Scott the next time my affection-tank is running low.

If you don't own a pet because you think it would add stress to your life, you might want to reconsider. According to a March 1996 Associated Press article coming out of Buffalo, New York, "When it comes to times of stress, researchers find, the most reassuring companion isn't your sweetheart—it's your schnauzer. A new study found that people who were put into stressful situations showed the least amount of tension when accompanied by their dog. The stress levels were highest when the subjects were with their spouses." I wouldn't suggest getting rid of your spouse and replacing him or her with a dog. But for your health and well-being you just might discover that caring for an animal, and having it care for you, might just turn out to be one of life's unexpected jubilees.

*Who provides food for the raven, when its young ones cry to God....Do you know the time when the wild mountain goats bear young? Or can you mark when the deer gives birth?...Who set the wild donkey free?... Have you given the horse strength?...Does the hawk fly by your wisdom? [Questions from God, the ultimate "pet owner," when He spoke out of the whirlwind to Job.]*

JOB 38:41; 39:1,5,19,26 NKJV

# 21

# Keep It Ridiculously Simple

Unless your life's been too complex to notice, you've probably observed that one of the major trends that went through Boomerville was labeled "voluntary simplicity." Truth be known, much of it was really involuntary simplicity, but our generation has its pride. We don't like to think of ourselves as being forced to simplify our lives because, say, our company's downsized and we've been laid off. Or that we went bankrupt from playing fast and loose with credit cards. We Baby Boomers prefer to see this as a voluntary exercise in freedom of choice.

One small tan book, *Simplify Your Life,* was near the forefront of this wave of cutting back, slowing up, paring down, opting out, and moving away to John Wayne-sounding places like Montana and Wyoming and the Texas hill country. In an interview with the *New York Times,* the author of this book and several get-rid-of-junk-in-your-life sequels, Elaine St. James, is quoted as saying, "I was sitting at my desk one day, and my schedule was full of phone calls and appointments and meetings with people, and I realized this was just not what I wanted to do." She continued, "I had finally reached a point I think many of us reach—of despair. We're tired of these complex lives and never having time to ourselves. I think the despair is coming from our souls' keep."

According to the article, Ms. St. James gave up her job in real estate, threw away masses of extra stuff, moved from a

3000-square-foot home to a 600-square-foot condominium. She even pared down her wardrobe to three basic colors: black, gray, and white. And get this, ladies: "She reduced her purse to a rubber band around a credit card, library card, license, and money."

I mentioned these facts to my friend Gracie over lunch recently.

"Well," Gracie commented, her fork punctuating the air, "I've about had it with all this talk of simplicity. It makes me feel way too guilty about wanting an interesting, busy life with reds and purples in my wardrobe. I think I'll write a book called *Complicate Your Life.*"

I have to admit, I could add plenty of personal material to Gracie's book concept. However, I do have a couple of simplifying tips of my own I could probably submit to Ms. St. James. Since she already has her own book, though, I think I'll just keep my ideas and share them with you. May I present "Becky's Hints for the Simple-Minded."

## On Matching Socks

In a word, don't. I'm telling you, trying to pair socks is a dead-end job. I know Nike's commercial says, "Just do it." But they are talking about shoes. They need a commercial for socks that says, "Don't bother." Sure, a tennis shoe is known to sneak off now and then (is that why they call them "sneakers?"), but it generally turns up after a few minutes of its owner's pawing under the couch.

Socks, on the other hand (or in this case, on the other foot), can't be trusted to stay faithful to one another even if you staple them, tie them in a knot, and have them repeat vows. I have no idea where their mates run off to or why they do it so quickly and permanently. (In desperation Erma Bombeck once told her children that missing socks "go to live with Jesus." I wonder if her kids pictured angels flying around heaven wearing a colorful array of mismatched socks). Since it seems socks are intent on staying single, my advice is, "Quit fighting them."

Our family has simplified our life by having one giant laundry basket (The Sock Single's Joint) where I dump all socks as they come out of the dryer. I mean everyone's socks: from Scott's dress socks to Rachel's ankle socks to Gabe's crusty, holey ones. In the morning, it is every sibling and spouse for himself (or herself, as the case may be). I usually just close my eyes and reach in the basket (as if it's a grab bag bin) and slip my cold feet into whatever I happen to pull up. Of course, I work at home where no one cares that I'm wearing an orange scrunch sock on one foot and a man's navy dress sock on the other.

## Organizing Silverware

I know this advice of mine may sound repetitive, but again my advice boils down to: Don't do it. Throw out those time-consuming little sorting trays and just dump the knives, forks, and spoons straight out of the dishwasher basket into an open drawer. In two seconds, the job's done. I actually owe this hint to my mother-in-law, Beverly. She's been dumping silverware haphazardly for years, and so far no one's stood at the drawer in a fit of confusion saying, "Will somebody help me? I simply can't tell a spoon from a fork if they aren't stacked together into neat little compartments." If someone in your family can't pick out the utensil they need from the rest of the bunch, they have more problems than presorting their flatware would solve.

## Cooking

My cousin Jamie wrote me a letter describing how she recently discovered a way to simplify the baking of goodies for her children.

She'd been buying packaged cookies for years, but eventually her children tasted The Real McCoy cookies:

homemade treats from Grandma's house. From that moment, they began begging Jamie to make some real, from scratch, sugar cookies. Jamie gave being Betty Crocker a valiant try but, alas, after the dough balls were placed in a hot oven, she discovered to her surprise that they melted and grew. When she opened the door to take a peek at her creation, the kids were distraught.

"We didn't want pancakes!" they cried. "We asked for cookies!"

Jamie consoled them and the next day she bought several beautiful cookies from the local bakery, spread them on a cookie sheet, and then—just a minute before the children came in the door from school—popped the whole thing in the oven to warm them. When she pulled the tray of confections out of the oven, thankfully, the children never asked any questions and Jamie only felt a slight twinge of guilt when she heard them bragging and sharing "our mom's homemade cookies" with the neighborhood kids.

## Birthday Gifts

I don't know if other people's children make a habit of this, but my children tend to put off telling me vital information until the very last minute. For example, last night around 5:30 P.M. as I was putting a pan of chicken into the oven, my youngest son burst through the back door shouting, "The PTO Spaghetti Supper and Meet the Teacher Night is tonight! It starts at 6:00!" That was a shock, but the most common last-minute fiascoes seem to revolve around birthday parties.

"Oh, Mom!" one of them will yell—generally about the time I've climbed into the shower and soaked and lathered my hair. "I have to be at Joshua's birthday party in 15 minutes!"

"Joshua has a birthday party today?!?" I yell back as I scurry to rinse the soap out. "Why didn't you tell me this sooner?"

"I forgot!" the panicky voice will shout through the door. "And we need to get him a present too!"

This scenario has repeated itself so often around our house that we've invented what we call "The Simplified Birthday Gift." Before we head out the door to the car, my hair still dripping wet, I'll instruct the kids to grab a ribbon and some crayons or markers. Then I drive to the nearest convenience store, ask the clerk for a brown paper bag and, working together as a team, we fill it up with assorted kid junk: bubblegum, Slow Pokes, gummy critters, Tootsie Rolls, taffy—if it will rot your teeth, it goes in the bag. After paying for the loot, we jump back in the car where the kids decorate the bag with the crayons and tie it all up with the ribbon. And there you have it—a generic all-purpose birthday gift, suitable for any sex or any age child. Their parents may not be thrilled with it, but it's a surefire hit with the recipients.

I'm guessing that about half the women (those of the creative, right-brained variety) who are reading this chapter will understand and applaud my hints for the simpleminded. The other half (the organized, logical ones) will worry about my sanity and the welfare of my children. That's understandable. Believe me, there are days when I too worry about my sanity and the welfare of my children. But then, every so often, something purely delightful happens that assures me I'm okay.

One night we'd had a bunch of teenagers, friends of our kids, over to our crazy house for the night. One of the teens, upon entering and seeing our laid-back home and the rock-climbing wall, exclaimed, "Wow, this is the most RANDOM house I've ever seen! Cool!"

The next day, another one of our boy's friends sent a note to me that said simply, "Becky, I love coming to your house."

My heart was warmed, until I read on...

"Because there's nothing we can do to mess it up."

*Seek ye first the kingdom of God and his righteousness; and all these things shall be added unto you.*

Matthew 6:33 kjv

## 22

# That Stuff Will Kill You

Food, glorious food!

When did it become so risky to eat it?

Am I the only one bewildered with counting calories, fat grams, sugar, and bran flecks? Just as soon as I got all the calorie counts memorized—of everything from a jelly donut (with and without glaze) to a ¼-inch sliced pickle—calories fell from nutritional grace. Now we have to find room in our overcrowded brains to store grams of fat. (Fat gram numbers, that is. Not cells.)

By now you may have noticed that scientists love playing a game with the general population called, "This Stuff Will Kill You." They come out with a new report showcasing the latest food that is destined to make us all keel over dead if we don't stop consuming it, and NOW.

A few months later—just to keep us alert and alarmed—the illustrious experts change the game plan.

"Come to think of it," a newsbreaking article will report, "maybe we were a bit hasty last year. Turns out that food we warned you about doesn't actually kill you. Is that what you thought we were saying? No, no, no. Actually, our latest research shows eating this particular item, in fact, may help you live to be well over 120. Sorry about the mix-up. But stay tuned, one and all, for our next round of 'This Stuff Will Kill You.'" By the time we've all suffered through months of withdrawals trying to disassociate our bodies from the so-called "deadly cuisine"—well, it's hard to see the humor in these little medical recants.

For example, having been so thoroughly warned about the dangers of ingesting caffeine, we stoically and collectively stumbled and snored our way through hundreds of mornings, sacrificing our beloved real coffee for blah, unleaded substitutes. About the time we were all falling asleep on our lunch trays, the scientists announced (I imagine with dastardly glee), "Woops—another boo-boo! Now we have found that the chemicals used to dissolve the caffeine are far more dangerous than drinking real Java. And by the way, a new study shows that one of the ten things centenarians have in common is that they all drank caffeinated coffee. And we've found—surprise, surprise—coffee actually makes you more attentive. Isn't this amusing?" Garfield the Cat spoke up for the nation when he responded with a wild-eyed poster yelling, "Give me COFFEE now—and no one will get hurt!"

These days strong coffee is not only back in favor, it comes in every flavor. It's the hip-happenin' beverage of the hour. I think the explosive popularity of Starbucks and other gourmet coffee shops may be the consumers' way of expressing our sheer gratitude for the return of the bean with caffeine. As long lines form behind foaming, spitting cappuccino machines, it's as though we're all paying silent homage. How we missed you, O Morning Cup of Fresh Brew! Welcome to our world again, Fresh Ground Hazelnut Beans. Never again will we take you for granted—see, you're practically royalty now.

Still, the nutritional community persists in its efforts to spoil the joy of most well-loved comfort foods. The mere thought of a warm mug of cocoa, or hot apple pie à la mode, or French fried onion rings makes us salivate. Until, that is, we hear doctors warn about the results on our hips and hearts. It's a national nutritional bummer!

There is, however, a grassroots revolt springing up that will be interesting to watch in coming years. In her book

*Clicking,* famed trend watcher Faith Popcorn points to a new phenomena she coins "Pleasure Revenge." Already "fat free" products are shown to be sliding off America's grocery lists. "Give us back real cream! Butter! Potatoes fried in oil!" cry the fat-starved masses. Why? According to *The Popcorn Report,* people have been depriving themselves of fat-laden goodies for several years and have not found their lives, on a whole, to be any more fulfilling (or "full-feeling," for that matter). You mean living fat-free was not the big key to perpetual bliss? Ah, well...back to the grocery shelf.

Thankfully, there seems to be some good news on this score for those of us who cherish our comfort cuisine and are trying to make peace with our bulging battles. Medical doctor David Sobel, along with his research partner, psychologist Robert Ornstein, asks: Is being thin worth the daily torture of deprivation, calorie counting, and rigid exercise regimens that it takes for most of us to maintain our ideal weight? "Probably not," they write. "In fact, being pleasingly plump is healthier than subjecting ourselves to the ups and downs of constant dieting. And while there is no question that what and how we eat is related to our heath, 'dieting is not a healthy way to eat.'" Yes! I want to shout. Pleasingly Plumps of the world unite! (Shall we celebrate by going out for cheesecake and real coffee?)

Leo Buscaglia is a speaker whose outlook on life I've often admired. I think it is because he's the epitome of a big-hearted Italian. (Somehow, I can't help but believe there's a passionate Italian serenading somewhere in my ancestors' genes.) In his book, *Bus 9 to Paradise,* Buscaglia bemoans the medical assault on his cherished family dishes such as "carbonara with proscuitto, butter, and cheese." Leo's mama, noting his distress, gave him some simple advice: "Have it all, but in moderation." Buscaglia's mother lived a happy life until the ripe old age of 82. "Not bad for a woman with high blood pressure and astronomical levels of cholesterol."

What about all the thin people who sound so well-meaning when they tell their fluffier friends, "I only want you to lose weight for your own self-esteem. It will give you a brighter outlook on life." "Oh, contrare," the well-rounded may now answer back with confidence, holding both chins high. Doctors Sobel and Ornstein also say that in spite of popular opinion, "fat people do not seem to have any greater psychological problems than do slim people. Some studies support a 'jolly-fat connection,' in which over-weight people show significantly less anxiety and depression than do their slimmer peers." Ho-ho-ho! Take that, smug speedy-metabolizers!

Just as I enjoy the variety of foods God's given us, I also love the variety and creativity He used in people-ing our planet. Short and tall, plump and skinny, all shades of skin colors, curly and straight hair, blue, green, and brown eyes. God even playfully decorated some of us with dimples and chocolate-sprinkle freckles. He gifted us with affectionate Down's syndrome kids and brilliant Einsteins, Olympic athletes and inspiring paraplegics like Joni Eareckson Tada. If there's one thing I will mount a soapbox against, it is the idea that there is one "ideal" we must all be or achieve to be worthy of acceptance.

Since finally coming to accept and appreciate the middle-aged body I've been given by my Creator, my focus, in recent months, has shifted from overemphasis on out-ward appearances to seeking simple ways to keep it healthy and feeling good. I really HATE being sick—and last year I had a whole series of months where I could not seem to get well.

I grew weary of seeing doctors. They would order yet one more round of antibiotics that would kill the infection, but the "bug zapper" would also murder some of the good bacteria in my system, setting up the need for counter-medication. It was a never-ending cycle, with stronger and stronger antibiotics being prescribed each time. Another side complaint: I'm one of those people prone with the latent virus that breaks out now and again into mouth ulcers. During these months of lowered immunity, my mouth was afire with them! Okay, I'll admit it wasn't bone cancer or anything, but those of you who've suffered through a mouth full of canker sores will sympathize.

I found the solution to my health problem in a most unlikely place: at the bottom of a pond.

**Bless the LORD...Who satisfieth thy mouth with good things; so that thy youth is renewed like the eagle's.**

PSALM 103:2,5 KJV

## 23

# Pond Scum for Dinner

In desperation, I stopped into a health food store one day, poured out my health troubles, and asked the owner if she had any suggestions.

She smiled and said, "It's really not complicated. Eat a variety of foods you like, especially fresh fruits and vegetables, and enjoy every bite—in moderation." (The wisdom of an Italian mama echoed across the health food counter.) Her classic "eat-your-vegetables" advice reminded me of a quote I'd clipped from the *Dallas Morning News*. A doctor of 33 years and author of *Doctor Generic Will See You Now* says, "I must admit, the vegetarians whom I treat have the lowest cholesterols, the fewest cancers, the smuggest expressions, and the greatest amounts of intestinal gas of any patients in my practice."

*I wish I liked to eat veggies better,* I moaned silently. *These days I only feel like a vegetable.*

"There is one more thing," the health lady continued. "Our soil has become so depleted of minerals over the years that I would suggest adding some densely packed "supergreen" food supplements to your diet. Today it takes 75 bowls of spinach just to equal the same amount of iron one bowl contained in 1948. One Senate document showed that 99 percent of Americans are deficient in minerals."

I thought about the wisdom and mercy of God in providing for a period of Jubilee for the ground—of letting the soil take time off to replenish itself. *Lord, what have we done to the earth—and our health—in the name of progress?*

The owner of the store broke my silent musing when she said, "My mom just had radiation treatments for cancer, so I began feeding her a daily 'green cocktail' of barley grasses and algaes. The doctors are amazed by her progress and the lack of severe side effects."

That did it. I walked out of the health food store with my prize in hand—a large jar of spirulina, a blue-green algae compressed into pills. Algae, I discovered as I researched with rising interest, is known as the most nutritious food on the planet. It has properties of both a plant and an animal cell, making it rich in nearly every known vitamin and mineral and amino acids (which make up protein molecules.) Since it's an easily digestible food, it's 98 percent assimilable. In other words, your body gets to keep the algae it eats, whereas much of the vitamin and mineral supplements we swallow and the animal protein we eat literally goes to waste.

I began taking four 500 mg tablets right away, and that's the dosage I continue to take to this day. Some people take as a little as 250 mg and some as many as 10 grams, depending on how much energy they need. I usually swallow "my pond food" in the morning—on a full or empty stomach, it makes no difference. After all, it's just like eating a bowl of packed-down spinach (only it's easier to face a few tablets at this hour of the day than a bowl full of greens).

Almost immediately I noticed I had more energy, especially in the late afternoon when I would routinely make my bleary-eyed stagger for a bed or couch. Now, if I have time for a nap and I'm tired, I enjoy it thoroughly. (As I've stated, I have a great affection for nap-time.) But it's nice to have enough energy to keep going when I can't slow down and stop. Even better, nearly all my health problems have disappeared. For me, this has been simplest way to stay well I've ever happened upon. I can forget which vitamins you are supposed to combine with what: It's so much simpler for me to just swallow a whole vitamin- and mineral-packed food and be done with it.

Scott, who once thought I was crazy for bringing home edible "green pond food," is now a regular Jolly Green Gent, though he prefers to "drink his greens." Every morning he takes a spoonful of "supergreen" powder (also purchased at the health food store) made from barley, wheat grass, chlorella (another chlorophyll-rich algae), brown rice, and kelp (yum, yum), stirs it into a glass of orange juice, and downs it with a satisfied, "Ahhhh." Just the dark green color of it makes the rest of the family gag, but Scott swears it has made all the difference in how he feels and says he can't taste the powder when it's dissolved in juice.

Keep in mind that neither Scott nor I are what you could even remotely call "health nuts." But we've happened upon something our bodies must have been missing, and it's worked so well for us that I want to share it with others just in case it might be of some help. We've not had as much as a cough or cold—even when everyone around us was succumbing to the flu and viruses. All of my infections cleared up—including the mouth sores—and I have had virtually no recurrences.*

More and more, as the cost of health care soars, we're taking preventive nutrition seriously. Many of you have probably already happened upon some kind of healthy regimen that seems to make a difference in how you feel. Leave it to me to develop an affinity for pond scum. But think about it, God designed algae to grow so easily and abundantly—in both fresh and salt water—that I can't help but wonder if it was originally created to be a food staple or some sort of supplement for man and animals. According to

---

\* For more information, see Notes.

experts, there's enough algae right now, waiting to be harvested, to feed the entire world several grams every day. And because it reproduces in mere HOURS, it is a never-ending food source.

To sum up my personal, down-home, back-porch food-simplifying remedy: Go ahead and have your occasional fried "Bloomin' Onion"! Dig heartily into your apple pie à la mode. Sip hot chocolate on your swing till the sun goes down. All in moderation. Just make sure that you get a nice order of pond food and wheat grass on the side. What could be simpler?

**To...*everything that has the breath of life in it—I give every green plant for food.***

GENESIS 1:30

## Me and Dr. Seuss

Someday, I may even write a children's book about the virtues of pond food. I thought I might title it *Green Algae and Ham* (with apologies to Dr. Seuss).

Would you like green food with ham?
Eat some pond scum, Sam-I-Am!
Would you eat it in a pill? Would you drink it when you're ill?
Would you sip it on a swing? Would you try it in the spring?
Try it, try it, you will see—a green and healthy jubilee!

## 24

# Diggin' and Prayin'

If we believe everything we read in the newspapers these days, we are a nation of really sick people. As a matter of fact, we have more infirm and afflicted than we have actual citizens. Columnist Bob Garfield recently added up all the millions of people who are supposed to be suffering from sickness (including 12 million Americans who suffer from "restless leg syndrome") and found the total comes to 543 million disease-ridden Americans "which means—in a country of 266 million people—either we as a society are doomed or someone is seriously double-dipping."

Even allowing for errors in addition, there are enough sick people around to make one feel queasy. What's the cure for all that ails us? Since I'm in charge of writing this book, I get to discuss the remedies that most strike my fancy. (Give me an inch...) I've already discussed my diet and pond scum supplement routine.

Next, I'd like to talk about exercise.

I love talking about exercise—it is actually doing it that I find so distasteful. Unless I'm getting "by the way" exercise. I love walking, for example, if I'm also shopping for bargains at the big outdoor market we East Texans know as First Monday. I enjoy calisthenics—when I'm doing deep knee bends and arm reaches while I'm in the process of trying on clothes in a department store dressing room. I don't mind aerobic dancing as long as I can do it while I'm sweeping and mopping the floor. But I do not have the time or inclination to drive 30 minutes in traffic, go to an exercise class for an hour, and subject my leotarded-lined body to public display just to let all that good energy out into thin air. By the time I drive back home I'm too tired to clean house or go shopping.

One day I met a woman I'd seen once before, but she looked much slimmer and more fit than when last we'd bumped into each other. "Wow!" I told her. "You look great! What have you been doing?" Her reply caught me off guard. "Digging a fishpond."

"Come again?" I asked.

"Well, I decided one day that I wanted a fishpond in my backyard. So I set out to dig one myself. By the time I'd dug the hole, laid the concrete, set the stones, filled it with gold-fish and water, and planted flowers around the edge—I got on the scales and I'd lost 20 pounds!"

"This is too good," I commented. "You know, together we could start the next health craze—The Fishpond Diet and Exercise Routine."

"Isn't it hilarious?" she giggled.

"I think it's great!" I responded enthusiastically. Then I began to wonder if there were some creative ways I could double up—you know, get fit and get something accomplished at the same time. I uncovered some interesting facts:

- A 120-pound woman (for those of you who are lucky enough to be one of them) burns 3 calories per minute making the bed or raking leaves (more than bowling or walking at 2 miles per hour).

- She burns 3.5 calories mopping (more than golf or riding horseback).

- 4 calories playing with children and scrubbing walls (same as playing doubles tennis).

- 4.2 mowing the lawn (only slightly less than playing half-court basketball).

- If you weed and dig in the garden, climb stairs, or like to dance to the radio, you'll burn up as many calories as backpacking, canoeing, skating, or chopping wood.

Whew! That's all the talk about exercise I can handle right now. I'm already feeling winded from the exertion.

Now here's my favorite health tip—perhaps the most effective of all: Prayer. There have been several breakthrough studies in recent years showing that prayer makes a positive difference in recovering health even when the sick people don't know that prayer is being made on their behalf. All other things being equal, a regular churchgoer, statistically speaking, will live longer than someone who has no regular place of worship. Believing is even better for you than was once thought, and the medical profession is finally beginning to take note—and kneel. Dr. Kenneth Cooper, the "father of aerobics," has recently written an entire book on the subject of how belief affects our bodies. Other prominent MDs are following suit.

When my children were small and their head ached or they had nightmares, inevitably they'd crawl up in my lap and ask me to pray for them (and when my head ached— I'd put my head in their tiny laps and ask them to do the same for me). I do not know how I would have survived their childhood illnesses without the soothing resource of prayer. (I'll never forget when the four of them had chicken pox one after another. I don't think I saw the light of day for two months!)

Once I began praying, their little bodies would relax and almost always they'd feel better. I have many memories of my mother and father praying aloud at my bedside when I was sick. I never questioned whether or not it would work. I simply relaxed, knowing my body would heal in God's time and that I was loved and cared for until then. To this day I know the prayers of four believing grandparents make a difference in my children's lives. How comforting it is to know that heaven is bombarded daily with prayers for our family. That our lives—in sickness and in health—are in His loving hands.

Now if you'll excuse me, I have to go do my laundry aerobics while I pray for my family at the same time. Hey, I could write the next bestseller, a combination book on spirituality and chores as exercise.

And I could call it *Pray 'n' Wash!*

*(Okay, enough already. I can hear you groaning from here!)*

**Is any one of you sick?... pray for each other so that you may be healed. The prayer of a righteous man is powerful and effective.**

JAMES 5:14,16

# Part V

# Green Pastures, Still Waters

*Answers That
Restore the Soul*

# 25

# Small Stuff

've found the woman I want to be—the woman who lives in my head but has not, as yet, found her way into my real life. But that's okay. Sometimes these things take time. The woman I want to be is well over 80 years old anyway, so I'm thinking perhaps it probably takes a long time to grow a balanced life. My new heroine is an artist. She wears long antique cotton dresses (with aprons), she dons a bonnet, she's barefoot, and she has twinkling eyes and a childlike, joyous, mischievous outlook on life. Her name is Tasha Tudor.

I've come to know Tasha Tudor only recently, but many of you may have already discovered this delightful treat of a lady through her illustrated children's books or in one of the beautifully photographed volumes about her life such as *Tasha Tudor's Garden.*

This Christmas our family was on the receiving end of an unexpected and incredible gift from my generous, book-loving, Southern belle friend, Ruby Katherine: three enormous boxes of new books. There were children's books, novels, devotionals, classics, dozens of hardback scrumptious reads—and among all that treasure were books about Tasha Tudor. For days after opening those boxes I was like a child let loose in a candy store, sampling bites of this book and nibbles of that, anxious to see if the filling tasted as good as the coating advertised. All the books were delightful, but thus far, the Tasha books are my favorites.

When I telephoned to thank Ruby Katherine and commented on the books I liked best, she replied, "Oh, Becky. I knew you'd love Tasha Tudor's books. Whenever I'm feeling frazzled and frantic I leaf through the beautiful pictures and relaxing words and—like osmosis—I absorb it all and find myself feeling calmed again."

During a recent visit with my little sister, Rachel, I asked if she'd ever heard of Tasha Tudor.

"Yes!" Rachel almost shouted, grabbing my arm in a gesture of excitement. "I have an interview with her on video that I'll have to send you. She's the cutest little thing. Sort of an ancient-looking, bird-like woman with a disarming sense of humor and an adorable voice. To her the littlest things are 'fun, quite entertaining, or delightful.' She even made being *old* sound like the best possible stage of life. I remember, at one point, the camera focused on Tasha as she sweetly painted away on her canvas, talking about how she always draws from real life instead of from still pictures. Then she said, 'I have a whole freezer full of little mice that I found in various places, wrapped in death. Would you like to see them?' It was hilarious to imagine this sweet, gentle lady thawing and re-freezing an entire morgue of woodland creatures to use as models for her book illustrations!"

"Do you think she's sort of eccentric then?"

"Yes, but in a really delightful, sane sort of way."

"Send me the video. I can always use one more happy, eccentric role model in my life."

My sister's package with the video arrived last week. Appropriately titled *Take Joy!*, I've already watched it over five times and still I'm not tired of it. There is so much about this woman that fascinates me. I'm not even completely sure of all the reasons. I certainly don't agree with some of her peculiar ideas about religion (she and her family made one up to their own liking, mostly as an excuse to have a feast and celebrate), but I wholeheartedly embrace her enthusiasm for the simple joys of life.

Tasha loves children, and it is obvious her own enchanting childhood is never far from her memory. She also loves animals (she has her milking goats, her beloved corgis, and a pet parrot who likes to play dead on the dinner plates); adores her lush flower and herb garden ("I haven't any modesty when it comes to my garden," she says, "I'll boast like mad."); and has a great affection for tiny things—dollhouses, miniature furnishings, and the like.

When her children were small, Tasha went to elaborate means to give them fun, happy memories. For example, each of her children had a miniature mailbox on their bedroom door. During the day, while they were at school, Tasha made the teeniest letters and tiny hand-decorated cards (no bigger than an inch and a half square) and slipped them into the mailboxes, telling her children they were from the doll family. They called this make-believe game "The Sparrow Post." Tasha even made a tiny catalogue so the children could order doll dresses and hats from it, paying for their orders with buttons. In a few weeks, the real clothes would arrive—her children never guessing that their mother was the seamstress.

Tasha contentedly admits to having accomplished one of the things most important to her: She gave her children blissful memories of their childhood. To this day she continues to make marionette puppets, write elaborate plays, and direct her children and grandchildren as they put on productions for the community. Having Tasha for a mother might have been better even than having Mary Poppins for a nanny and Pippi Longstocking for a next-door neighbor.

Contemplating this caused me to pause and ask myself a difficult question: "What sort of memories will my own children have of their childhood and, in particular, of their mother?" I wasn't sure, so I sought out my youngest son and inquired of his thoughts on the matter.

"What will I remember most?" Gabe asked, repeating my question as we drove along in the car—picking up and delivering various siblings from play practice, basketball, and youth group activities. "I'll tell you what I remember: laughing and laughing. In the car. You're always saying the funniest things or laughing at something we said or running over a curb. Yep. I'll remember watching the back ends of cars in front of us, and laughing, and telling you what I want to order at the drive-through." Hmmm...not too shabby a memory—all things considered.

I'm sure my children will have memories of a family in too much of a hurry, but, hopefully, they'll also remember laughter echoing over idling engines. For I realize all too well, it is the little things that go into a Child's Memory Bank.

Toward the end of *Take Joy!* the narrator quotes a poem by Evelyn Underhill, one of Tasha's favorites. There is a phrase in that poem I keep running over in my mind as one would a smooth pebble in a pocket.

"'I come in the little things,' saith the Lord."

It is true we shouldn't sweat the "small stuff" in terms of negativity. But when it comes to joy, it's the small stuff that makes the world go 'round and infuses our life with meaning. Practice seconds of celebration, mini-Sabbaths, small pauses where you stop for a moment to say, "Thank you" for little things.

The sound of the laughter of a child.

The sun warm on your shoulders.

The smell of fresh coffee.

The taste of a sweet ripe peach.

The sight of a perfect red rose.

Mercy drops and showers of blessings are always falling around us. To miss these small accumulated joys is to miss God's gentle voice in our everyday lives. Pause for just a second to be grateful for something tiny but warm, delicious, and good in your life. See, then make it a habit. Don't miss your chance to reach out and take joy!

*Hear, O earth, the words of my mouth...as the small rain upon the tender herb, and as the showers upon the grass.*

Deuteronomy 32:1,2 KJV

## 26

# Grace Always Wins

Scott, in his matter-of-fact style, once said something profound. (He's probably said something profound more than once; it's just that this one quote stands out.) He said, "Most Christians I know who think they are being persecuted for their faith aren't being persecuted for their faith. They are being persecuted for being obnoxious."

Are some of us trying so hard to be good we're forgetting to be kind? It's like the young child who prayed, "Oh, God, make all the bad people good, and make all the good people nice." How often are Christians losing our "fight for the right" because we lack a spirit of love in how we communicate our views to the world? I see this not only in politics and the church at large, but, I'm ashamed to admit, I often see this attitude creeping into my own life. Unfortunately, this is what keeps relationships from experiencing more Jubilees—times of refreshment and forgiveness— when we find a relaxed joy in each other's company.

I've noticed that often it is bright, intelligent people who are most vulnerable to falling into the trap of one-up-manship. You know the type. They seem to be on constant Debate Mode, ready to nail any wrong to the wall in a single verbal blast. It must be hard for them. They know all the answers, so how can they let untruths slide by undebated? But what, and where, does it get them? Where is the taste of victory when there's no one to cheer—everyone's pinned to the wall, busy licking their puncture wounds?

The old saying is powerfully true: No one cares what you know unless they know that you care.

He who is most gracious wins.

When I allow this truth to sink into my head, my neck muscles relax, my fists unclench, and I realize that even if I am in the right, I will ultimately lose what's really important if I let my desire to win take over my ability to show love.

We once had a Sunday school teacher, Ed Wichern, who never ceased to impress me. His gracious manner endeared him to every person in our class. The thing that really amazed me was that Ed remained ever patient, kind, and gentle with a class filled with some pretty radical, sharp-tongued, and off-the-wall people (present company sometimes included). When someone in the class blurted out something wrong—completely off base—it was an incredible lesson in human relations to watch Ed at work. He thoughtfully nodded in the dissenter's direction, affirming them as a person worthy of love, and generally said something on the order of, "Isn't God good? We don't know all the answers, and yet we can rest in the fact that He loves every one of us in spite of our differing opinions." Then he deftly turned in his Bible to the next verse.

This operation reminded me of a skillful parent replacing a china cup with a plastic toy—the exchange occurring so swiftly and smoothly the toddler forgoes his usual tantrum. Ed has expertly diverted more than his share of Adult Sunday School fits.

The late Dr. Francis Shaeffer was one of the greatest Christian thinkers of this century. This apologist, philosopher, theologian, historian, and student of art, music, and politics spent his life arguing the logical case for the validity of Christianity in our modern world. And yet he was amazingly gracious and humble in the midst of debate and discussion—especially in his later years. Gentle eyes peered out of his elflike face. He customarily wore knickers, knee socks, and soft knit shirts rather than intimidating three-piece suits. When my parents were in their 30s struggling in their own search for Ultimate Truth, they were drawn to Schaeffer's works and eventually spent time studying under his teaching at L'Abri (meaning "The Shelter") in the mountain village of Huemoz, Switzerland. Love ruled Francis Schaeffer's words in writing and debate as it did his life.

In the late 1970s Scott and I, along with thousands of others, attended Schaeffer's breakthrough "How Should We Then Live?" conference in Dallas. My young collegiate head was pounding with all the information we were given. The brain power floating around that auditorium was palpable. During a question and answer session one afternoon, a particularly obnoxious (and possibly mentally ill) young man took the microphone and blasted an incoherent question toward Schaeffer. *What will Dr. Schaeffer do with this one?* I wondered as I fidgeted around in my chair. *He's really in up to his knickers now.*

In short, the crowded auditorium witnessed Love in Action. Schaeffer poured the love of God on this confused young man, diffusing him of anger. It was like watching a balloon released of its air. Years of patiently working with people had taught Dr. Schaeffer when it was time for intellectual/theological arguments and when it was time for simply sharing God's love. According to an article in *Christianity Today* (March 1997), Francis tended to be more sharp-tongued in his early years of ministry. "But in later years, wounds inflicted and received spurred him to serious reflection about how to handle theological disagreement in a spirit of genuine Christian love."

I recently read with great interest that Bishop Pike, the priest who became famous for his venture into the world of the occult, was involved in two debates toward the end of his life. The first debate pushed Pike further away from Christianity—in part, because of the opponent's obnoxious attitude. But in the second debate his opponent was Dr. Francis Schaeffer, who touched not only Bishop Pike's mind but also his heart. On the day Bishop Pike died, he was making plans to visit Dr. Schaeffer at his mountain home in Switzerland. I don't know who won the debate, but I know who won lasting respect.

Without love, even the soundest of theories are nothing but hollow, meaningless words thrown at others who may go away challenged, but untouched and unchanged. Love, expressed in kindness, permits us to unfold.

Yes, he who is most gracious wins.

### *Words from a wise man's mouth are gracious.*

ECCLESIASTES 10:12

## 27

# Letting Go to Be Free

From my back porch one summer morning I watched an object lesson unfold like some sweet story in a children's book.

The evening before, my children had found a baby blue jay struggling (and failing) to fly from the grass. To save the little foundling from becoming dog food, they picked it up and brought the tiny creature to me. It opened its wide mouth expectantly. When it didn't get the desired worm right away, it began to chirp. Incessantly. So I mixed up some baby cereal with a little water and tried to feed the poor orphan. The results of our feeding time were similar to what happened when I tried to give my own babies their first spoonful of Pablum. More cereal landed on beak and feathers and the front of my shirt than went down the hungry throat of the baby bird. *There's more to being a mother bird than I bargained for,* I thought to myself.

Finally, exhausted from effort, both the bird and I fell asleep. The next morning I awoke to a sharp series of chirp, chirp, chirps. "Look, little guy," I said loudly over his chirping, "I'd love to help you more than anything. But I just don't know how. Let's go look for your mama." I took my little noisemaker outside and balanced him carefully on the porch rail. Then I walked back inside the house and watched him from the sliding glass door. "Please, Lord," I prayed. "Bring help!" I could still hear the pitiful chirps through the glass.

Within a few seconds, the glorious sight of a mother bird flew into view. She coaxed the baby to follow her off the porch and up onto the safety of a nearby limb. "Yes!" I cheered from my observation point. "You can do it. Your mom's here now. Fly!" At that moment I spied a black and white cat slinking across the yard, looking exactly like Sylvester the cartoon cat. My heart stopped. My little "Tweety Bird" bird was a wobbly flyer at best. One false move and he would be breakfast.

Suddenly, a streak of blue plummeted from the sky and attacked the stalking cat. Was it a plane? Was it Superman? No—it was Daddy Bird to the rescue! I laughed in delight as I watched the big blue jay tease and divert the attention of the cat long enough for Mama Bird to get Baby Bird to a higher perch. I smiled, satisfied with the world, as I watched the family fly off together, leaving Sylvester still lickin' his frustrated chops.

Not audibly, but still plainly, I felt God saying to me, "This was My lesson for you today, Becky. You are a fixer by nature. You enjoy the strokes you receive from helping others—from saving them. But guess what? You can't fix everything that goes wrong and everyone who is hurting. Sometimes all you need to do is let go. Stand and watch while I take care of the job. I have plenty of Mama and Daddy Birds in My kingdom who are often more qualified to help than you are. Your job in solving many problems is to simply to let go, watch, and pray."

Catherine Marshall came to a similar place in her spiritual walk when she practiced what she called a prayer of relinquishment. On the morning of September 14, 1943, tired of wrestling and begging God to heal her, she said, "I'm beaten through, God. You decide what You want for me." She went on to say that "tears flowed. I had no faith as

I understood faith, expected nothing. The gift of my sick self was made with no trace of graciousness."

And the result? "It was as if I had touched a button that opened windows in heaven; as if some dynamo of heavenly power began flowing. Within a few hours I had experienced the presence of the Living Christ in a way that wiped away all doubt and revolutionized my life. From that moment my recovery began." Her conclusion was that "God absolutely refuses to violate our free will; that, therefore, unless self-will is voluntarily given up, God cannot move to answer prayer."

Voluntarily giving up? Letting go. How many areas could I apply this to my life—and possibly find the peace I'd been seeking? I could let go of having to meet everyone's needs. I could let go of the feeling that I'm solely responsible for keeping the house clean—and delegate chores! I could ask for all kinds of help in areas where I'm not gifted—organization, discernment—and not feel guilty for my shortfall. I could give my children and their future up to God! I could quit trying to figure out how to make the perfect marriage and give it to God instead. Jubilant thoughts flowed like a river unleashed.

Let's see, I could let go of perfection. Yes! I could let go of my need of approval!

I once heard a man ask an audience, "What risks would you take? What would you do if you let go of seeking the approval of man?" I let those two questions ring in my head over and over again for days. I realized I'd feel truly free, perhaps for the first time in my life, if I began to live for God's approval and gave up my gnawing need for the applause of others. "Do your work heartily, as to the Lord, rather than to men" became a daily reminder, a place to refocus my day. One by one, God seems to be leading me through experiences that teach me to let go of all my sources of approval—including the approval of my friends, my audiences (both my reading and listening audiences), and finally, perhaps, even the approval of my parents. Though I dearly love and respect them, I've found new freedom in letting go of needing their okay on everything I decide to do or choose to believe.

I could let go of grudges and deep disappointments. Author Anabel Gilham tells people to do this letting go in a visual and memorable way. She suggests taking a helium-filled balloon and an indelible marker and going off alone to a quiet place, like a park. Write whatever it is you need to let go of—burdens, bitterness, whatever is weighing you down—on the balloon (you may want to use a code between you and God). Then release it to God. Let the balloon go and watch it taken up into the sky until it disappears.

A couple of years ago, baseball great Mickey Mantle died after a long battle with liver disease—a result of years of alcohol abuse. Before his death, there were several stories circulating that he made his peace with Christ during the last year of his life. His funeral made the front page of the *Dallas Morning News*. Now I've never been a big fan of baseball, but when I saw the front page picture of a little boy—about age seven—sitting on a curb, head down, wearing a shirt with Mickey's number on it, I was touched. Who wouldn't be?

I scanned the article quickly, but one phrase caught my eye. So much that I put it to memory. The reporter wrote, "And in the end, his fans forgave him for being human." As I take in the view from Life's front porch, and mentally see the parade of friends and family that have come and visited and gone on their way, I see their faults and fears and failures. I know they also see mine. Yet as long as we are stuck in this place "with skin on," we have a choice to make. Will we hold our humanity against ourselves, or will we, in the end, let go of judgment—and forgive each other for being human? It doesn't take a genius to figure out which choice brings more peace. But it helps to be reminded by a little boy, sitting on the curb, shedding tears of love for a fallen hero whose feet were made of clay.

The time of Jubilee was a time of healing and celebrations for many reasons, but perhaps none more important than the rituals of letting go. Slaves and prisoners were set free, debts were forgiven, families once divided were to return home to unite again as a clan. It was the ultimate "clean slate experience."

When Jesus made His first public proclamation and revealed who He really was, the moment was both dramatic and palpable. After returning from a time of testing in the desert, Jesus went to His boyhood town of Nazareth. On the Sabbath day, someone handed Him the scroll of the prophet Isaiah. Jesus carefully unrolled the parchment and found the place He wanted to read.

"The Spirit of the Lord is on me, because he has anointed me to preach good news to the poor. He has sent me to proclaim freedom for the prisoners and recovery of sight for the blind, to release the oppressed, to proclaim the year of the Lord's favor" (Luke 4:18,19).

A hush settled over the synagogue. Everyone's eyes were riveted to this powerful, gracious man, Jesus. He began His sermon that morning—after the reading of Scripture—by saying, "Today this scripture is fulfilled in your hearing" (verse 21).

What did this mean? And what does it have to do with this book about Jubilee? Everything. "The year of the Lord's favor," according to Hebrew scholars, is simply another term for the Year of Jubilee. What this means, to us, is that

Jesus came as a ransom to buy back our freedom. As the praise song says, "Jesus is our Jubilee."

He frees us—like trapped birds to the heavens—from whatever cages of sin we are in.

That's about the sum of it. Like some sweet story from a children's book. Jesus rescued us, His children, in order to set us free—in every conceivable area of our lives. The greatest of all Jubilees.

Your Father's here. Now fly!

**Look at the birds of the air; they do not sow or reap or store away in barns, and yet your heavenly Father feeds them. Are you not much more valuable than they?**

MATTHEW 6:26

# No, I Won't Take Off
# My Rose-Colored Glasses

It only makes sense to fill my mind with the Goodness of God
To leave the hard questions in His hand
To trust He sees the Big Picture, when I don't

To fill my ears with music that soars and honors love
To fill my mind with Scripture, great books, vivid poetry—
courageous, joyful, dancing words
To fill my eyes with the smiles of children,
And watercolor sunsets

To fill my senses with the sound of my Love's voice,
And the touch of his skin
To spend time with those who have been seasoned
with warmth and wisdom—
Who've walked a long time with the Friend of Friends
To fill these walls with laughter splashing over,
So that our home beckons, "Come and Join!"

If I don't, the World will surely fill the empty spaces in my head
With unrelenting news of violence, hate, and destruction—
And when I'm worn to the ground in despair
How can I help those who need me most?
If my cup is not full of Light—
What will I have to share
With those who cry out in their Darkness?

No, I won't take off these Rose-Colored Glasses
I work too hard to keep them on.

**Becky Freeman**
Copyright © 1994

# Notes

### Chapter 3—Natural Woman

Page 36: "Every person needs..."; "Each person deserves..."; "If we step..."
Maya Angelou, *Wouldn't Take Nothing for My Journey Now* (New York: Bantam Books, 1994).

### Chapter 8—Relaxing with Our Flaws

Page 79: "I fondly accept..."
Enid Howarth and Jan Tras, *The Joy of Imperfection* (Minneapolis: Fairview Press, 1996).

### Chapter 10—In Search of Joy Triggers

Page 97: "Instead of grabbing life..."
Roz Van Meter, *Passion!: Reclaiming the Fire in Your Heart* (Dallas, TX: Hollingsworth Press, 1994).
Page 97: "Less Wild God"
Brent Curtis and John Eldredge, *The Sacred Romance: Drawing Closer to the Heart of God* (Nashville, TN: Thomas Nelson, Inc., 1994).

### Chapter 11—Music to Soothe the Savage Mom

Page 106: "Far in the distance..."
Corrie ten Boom, *Tramp for the Lord* (East Rutherford, NJ: Jove Publications, Inc., 1986).

### Chapter 13—For the Beauty of the Earth

Page 117: "We have an appetite..."
Robert Ornstein and David Sobel, *Healthy Pleasures* (Portland, OR: Perseus Press, 1990).
Page 119: "Evening is for sharing..."
Anne Morrow Lindbergh, *Gift from the Sea* (Westminster, Maryland: Pantheon Books, 1991).

### Chapter 16—Holy Work

Page 137: "Jesus kept laying his hand..."
Source unknown.

### Chapter 18—Writing Back to Life

Page 143: "Tell me this..."; "Of course I would..."
Lucy Maud Montgomery, *Emily of New Moon* (New York: Bantam Books, 1983).
Page 144: "So the rejection..."
Madeleine L'Engle, *A Circle of Quiet* (San Francisco: HarperSanFrancisco, 1986).
Page 145: "You mean life is more..."
Susanne Lipsett, *Surviving a Writer's Life* (San Francisco: HarperSanFrancisco, 1994).
Page 146: "I know some very great..."
Anne Lamott, *Bird by Bird* (Two Harbors, MN: Anchor Books, 1995).

### Chapter 19—Gourmet Napping

Page 158: "He would doze off in a chair..."
Paul Kaufman, contr., Michael Ray, contr., Daniel P. Goleman, *The Creative Spirit* (New York: Plume, 1993).

### Chapter 21—Keep It Ridiculously Simple

Page 167: "I was sitting at my desk..."
Elaine St. James, *Simplify Your Life* (New York: Hyperion, 1994).

### Chapter 22—That Stuff Will Kill You

Page 175: "Probably not. In fact..."
Robert Ornstein and David Sobel, *Healthy Pleasures* (Portland, OR: Perseus Press, 1990).

### Chapter 23—Pond Scum for Dinner

Page 181:

Because it has been several years since I wrote this chapter on algae, I have had dozens of people write and ask, "What brand do you use?" "Do you still take it?" "What about reports of toxicity in some algae?"

First, yes, we still take it every day—and find our colds and infections are almost nil. I use Earthrise brand (www.earthrise.com) because it is raised in a controlled environment, eliminating the occasional toxicity problem from wild blue-green algae harvested from lakes.

My interest in natural supplements, along with the entire nation's growing interest in natural preventative health, continues to grow and blossom. For anyone suffering from mental, physical, or emotional disorders, I (along with their physicians and other counselors) highly recommend seeing a certified naturopath or MD familiar with nutritional therapies. Over the years I have consistently received more help from qualified nutritionists than I ever have from medical doctors, though I usually try both, just to make sure all bases are covered.

More and more I'm convinced that our weight, energy, and digestive problems are a result of the lack of nutrition in our foods—and often the result of antibiotic over-use, which produces candida overgrowth, causing havoc to just about every system in our bodies if left unchecked. Vitamins, minerals, amino acids, and herbs—when given under the care of a qualified health practitioner at therapeutic doses—can do WONDERS without side effects for most people.

You may want to check the following resources which have proven to be helpful, nutrition-based resources for those wanting to try alternatives to standard drug treatment therapy for a variety of problems:

1. For ADD/ADHD: <www.bcalmd.com>

2. For Bipolar Disorder: <www.truehope.com>

3. For alcohol or drug abuse/emotional disorders/sugar craving/tobacco craving: <www.healthrecovery.com>

Even if you or someone you love doesn't have an addiction or serious disorder, the books *Seven Weeks to Sobriety* and *Seven Weeks to Emotional Health,* recommended on this Web site, are enormously insightful. The author lost her teenage son to suicide after a bout with depression resulting from his inability to overcome an addiction. This experience sent her in desperate search of "What's happened?" and "What can we do to help these kids?" It's a breath of fresh air for those with loved ones struggling to overcome addictions, as well as all of us who struggle with everyday cravings and energy/emotional slumps.

After reading the book *The Craving Brain* a few years ago, I became convinced that it is nearly impossible for human beings to stop a strong craving on our own, and the author alluded to some future hope that scientists would discover what is missing in certain body chemistries that cause cravings for everything from cigarettes to chocolate.

Encouraging new research suggests that people with addictions to sugar, tobacco, and alcohol all have a sugar-based craving problem because alcohol is made from sugar and tobacco is cured with 75 percent sugar. Part of the puzzle to stop cravings appears to be amino acid/vitamin therapy. In fact, the success rate for people losing weight and getting off substance abuse is amazingly high when coupled with a targeted nutritional supplement program. Check out <www.healthrecovery.com> for more information on this.

4. Alzheimer's/Forgetfulness: *Brain Longevity* by Dharma Singh Khalsa, MD

5. Weight Problems/PMS Symptoms: *Your Hidden Food Allergies Are Making You Fat* by Dr. Rudy Rivera, MD

This book also has valuable information on candida overgrowth. If you suspect this may be a problem for you, particularly if you are having digestive problems, read *The Yeast Connection* as well. I go to Dr. Rivera, who has a practice in Plano, Texas—and he's been a remarkable help with PMS symptoms, weight struggles, and general health. I'm feeling and looking better than I have in years.

### Chapter 27—Letting Go to Be Free

Pages 200-201: "I'm beaten through…"; "It was as if I had touched…"
Catherine Marshall, *To Live Again* (Grand Rapids, MI: Chosen Books, 1996).